BLACKBOOK

CREATE THE BUSINESS
THAT YOU HAVE DREAMED.

The **Ultimate Guide** to Starting a Clothing Line

BLACKBOOK

By: David A. Codamo

Welcome to
contents

INTRODUCTION

Work hard every day and like your job.

Congratulations on taking the first steps to creating a successful clothing line! You are reading this book because you are ready to start a business selling t-shirts, hats, outerwear, accessory goods, and more. Well, you have made the right choice. Selling clothing goods is one of the most satisfying ways to make money these days and it is an awesome way to express your creativity and communicate your passion to others. Imagine walking down the street or through the mall and suddenly you notice the person in front of you is wearing one of your products. How satisfying would that feel? Somebody is wearing your creative ideas and believes in your vision strongly enough to pay good money for it!

It's great to be excited about exploring this new world of entrepreneurship, but keep in mind that you may not start out by being successful overnight. Success is a process; it takes many little steps, clear goals, and multiple achievements before the hard work pays off, literally! No company has started up and immediately become the next Diamond Supply Company, Supreme, or Huf. However, with some hard work, good advice, and a few unique creative ideas, you can actually set yourself firmly on the path to incredible success.

LEARNING CURVE AHEAD

If you are ready to put in the hard work to reap the benefits and rewards of running a successful t-shirt business, then it is time to start a new learning curve. Making t-shirts isn't easy, but with the right tools and access to the right information, your job can be a little easier. Whether the new information you need is to learn how to draw t-shirt designs, or you have no idea how to analyze the competition in your targeted market, or how to control and manage expenses, then this book is definitely for you.

OVERNIGHT SUCCESS? THINK AGAIN!

The biggest question I am asked these days is, "how did you get started?". Here's a brief overview. When I was younger, my family couldn't afford all the cool new toys, the name brand clothes, or the latest Air Jordans. I was always interested in how things were made, so I decided in high school to pursue the field of design. I hoped to go to college and learn about creating new ideas. Long story short, I finished college with a Bachelors Degree in Science for Product Design and Development.

During college I started doing freelance design work for clients, creating products, designing logos, and building websites. At last I was making a little money so I could buy all the clothes and name brands I couldn't have as a kid.

About that time I noticed a huge increase in the popularity of streetwear and indie clothing companies. I started reading the success stories of clothing entrepreneurs like Johnny Cupcakes, Benny Gold, and Nicky "Diamond" Tershay. Hearing their stories of hard work and success motivated me to learn everything I could about the industry and how I could create my own success.

I wanted to build something positive; I wanted to establish a brand that had solid meaning at its foundation. I started by searching for words that expressed my values. Eventually I came up with the name, "**Gold Deeds.**"

GOLD is considered precious, beautiful, highly valued, and of the most superior quality. I'm sure you've heard of the gold standard, or the expressions "a heart of gold" and "your weight in gold." That's the idea. **GOLD** is the individual that has empowerment.

DEEDS are notable and praiseworthy actions you perform in the service of your community and your life. **DEEDS** can be small or major achievements. Your **DEEDS** could involve music, dance, laughter, listening, sports, education, or other actions you perform daily or time to time in your life.

GOLD DEEDS is taking pride in who you are and what your good at. They are the expression of your talents and skill sets at whatever it maybe. This standard is what motivates you and reminds you to be ambitious and drives you to pursue success. **GOLD DEEDS** embraces your self-worth and invites you to challenge yourself; to be "worth your weight in gold" and to know that you are "**GOLD From Day One**"

I started by creating some logo samples and design ideas and showing them around to friends. I received good feedback and made a few samples. Started wearing the samples at school, at the gym, and when I went out.

People started asking where I got the cool shirts and where they could buy them. That's when I knew I could possibly have a good thing going, so I ran with it! Found a screen printer, ordered a few shirts, sent out text messages, posted on Facebook to friends and started selling.

The rest is history. Not quite! It's been a very long road to success. Long nights, lack of sleep, tons of research, and a whole lot of trial and error. But that's why I created the T-shirt Black Book.

The T-shirt Black Book is the ultimate resource for startup entrepreneurs who want to learn how to create a clothing line, a successful one! It started with me answering questions I was sent online. It grew into helping thousands of individuals build their dream businesses and achieve financial freedom. Now I've decided to put it all together in one place. My goal is to provide you with some in-depth, relevant content. I want to give you tools you can use today to kickstart your clothing business!

LET'S BE REALISTIC

CHAPTER 01

Before you start thinking about what you're going to be spending your millions of dollars on, you have to understand very clearly that it is going to take a lot of time, effort, and hard work to even come close to the potential of running even a slightly successful t-shirt business. Business owners and entrepreneurs at the top of the clothing industry will even tell you this, "you are entering a market dominated by competitors". You will encounter some huge businesses that would take every customer that would even think about coming to your business, and not even blink! Yes, it is a cruel world out there to see what big business will do for profit.

But, it's not all bad news. Provided that you are dedicated to your business, and have a strong desire for success, customers will eventually become loyal to you and what your brand stands for. Just keep producing a quality product, and build up a brand that people can trust then you will be on the right track to success.

DO YOU HAVE WHAT IT TAKES TO MAKE IT?

Being an entrepreneur is not easy. The primary trait needed when pursuing any business venture is self-motivation. Your business isn't going to start, and operate by itself. There will be times when you do not feel like working on your business or you're too tired. The problem is, if you're not working on your business, than who is? That's right, nobody!

Day after day you will need to keep your focus and your efforts trained on each aspect of your business, even when you don't feel like it. That's where self-motivation is extremely important! Treat your business like a newborn baby, a baby that is hungry all the time and never wants to be left alone. Sure, all your hard work will pay off down the road, but "down the road" is not now. Now is the time to hustle!

Self-motivation, hard work, and dedication are not the only factors required to launch a successful t-shirt business. You also need something just as important: money. T-shirt businesses are expensive when you first start out. Many people give up after just a few months, not realizing that in only a few more weeks they would have experienced their big financial breakthrough. The important thing to remember here is that you must devote yourself completely to your stated goal: to run a successful business.

Before you dive in, truthfully ask yourself if you have a passion strong enough to carry you through the difficult beginning phase. Are willing to devote most of your time and energy to producing t-shirts and clothing? If you pursue this route, your new business will eat up most of your free time. Watching Netflix, spending time with your family and friends, and other pleasant activities well be replaced by time spent building your business. Are you truly ready to sacrifice that time, spending it instead on your business?

If you are not all that devoted to making and selling t-shirts, or if you have the unrealistic expectation that you will become a millionaire overnight, then perhaps the clothing business is not for you. If, however, you do have a passion and a desire to accomplish something bigger than yourself, then keep reading.

EVERYBODY HAS TO START FROM SOMEWHERE

CHAPTER 02

Before we get into the more complicated details of starting a t-shirt business, we are going to look at the 10 most important tips to help you on our journey.

THE 10 MOST IMPORTANT TIPS FOR STARTING A T-SHIRT BUSINESS

1. RESEARCH ALWAYS COMES FIRST

Would you be able to fly a plane without first learning what it takes to fly one? Then, how do you think you are going to run a t-shirt business without knowing how to start and run any business?

Research is always the most important step when it comes to starting something new. The more research you do and the better you can absorb and understand the details of the industry, the easier it will be to answer the hard questions when they come up. It is essential that you figure out how to market, sell, and specifically, how to make sales happen.

2. EVERYTHING MUST BE PLANNED IN ADVANCE

If you want to be successful, you have to understand exactly what you are going to do to become successful. Careful planning can never be dismissed. The soundness of your plan is one of the most important assets a business owner can ever possess.

You must have a plan for everything, including what t-shirts you will be making, who you will be selling them to, what are your long-term performance goals, what strategies you will use to get there, how you plan to market your business and your products, and so on. But, the most important question to ask yourself is...

3. WHO ARE MY COMPETITORS?

Apart from already established businesses, who in your local market are you competing against? Look for similar companies that started up in the last 3-5 years, not competitors that have been around for over a decade. For example, if you are making only blue t-shirts, what other businesses in your local area are selling blue t-shirts? How can you make yours better than theirs, and/or less expensively? The internet is a great tool to monitor current trends; it allows you to see what is popular and to tap into what could be the next popular product.

4. PEOPLE BUY ONLY WHAT THEY ACTUALLY WANT

Are you going to buy a carton of milk if you already have five gallons in the fridge? Probably not. The same applies to your customers. If you are selling a t-shirt they don't need, they don't find appealing or think it is not up to their standards, then they will not buy from you.

It's good to look at what's popular and selling, but don't make the mistake of copying someone else's successful idea. If you're doing what they have already done, then you're already a step behind. Plan for future trends.

5. EVERYTHING COSTS MONEY

It is everybody's dream to be a billionaire or to have a never-ending supply of money, but for most people, they are light-years away from ever getting close to that dream. My advice in a nutshell: always watch what you spend and have tools in place to help you manage your money.

Costs add up quickly in a t-shirt business and most of them are unexpected. Things like marketing, bags, boxes, storage, tags, labeling, and the all-important website are expenses that are separate from the actual costs of buying and printing the t-shirts. You need to know what your total costs are per t-shirt in order to work out how much you need to sell them for to make a decent profit.

6. EXPANSION THROUGH PROMOTIONS AND ADVERTISING

Whether you employ an advertising agency, the local newspaper, Facebook, Instagram, or even a radio station to promote your business, it is important that you put a lot of quality time and effort into ensuring that your marketing strategy is effective and actually reaches your targeted customer base. Plan to set aside a decent amount of money for marketing because, apart from buying products and inventory, this is the most important area of your business. While the costs are considerable, marketing has the potential to make you a lot of money in return. This is a case where it takes money to make money.

7. THEY SAY 3 IS A CROWD

Not true in this case. The more people you can find who are willing to help you create, manage, and grow your business, the better. Friends and family may have a strong desire to help you grow your vision. Perhaps you know of other business owners who could use your help in exchange for helping you reach your goals. Just make sure the people you ask for help are as passionate about your idea as you are. Also, if you bring on a business partner, make sure that person has talents and skills that you lack. That way, you can each work from your strengths and help each other with your weaknesses.

8. KNOW WHERE YOU ARE GOING

You wouldn't drive in the dark without your lights on, so how can you run a business if you don't know where it's heading? Whether you plan out how many t-shirts you want to sell in a week, or determine how many different designs you plan to make in a year, it is important to set clear goals for your business. Even if you don't reach those goals, at least you will have some benchmarks in place, to help you see why you didn't reach them. Based on that assessment, you will be able to apply different (and hopefully better) strategies for your next set of goals. As the saying goes, "if you can believe it, you can achieve it."

9. NEVER GIVE UP

As I stated before, some people quit too soon, not realizing that if they had hung on for just a few more weeks, they would have been successful. Starting a new and challenging business is all about patience and trusting that you will be rewarded for your efforts. It's just like college; you pay to go to college for two to four years (or more), but you do this to get a degree that will in return allow you to make more money than before you went to school.

Business is the same way. You have to put time and money into your business, as well as a bunch of hard work. Only after all this effort will you start to see a return on your investment.

If your business is struggling, stop and ask some questions to analyze the situation. Perhaps you are offering your products to the wrong group of customers, or maybe you are charging too much. It's also possible you just need to rework your designs. One incredibly useful tool is to ask your customers what they want in a t-shirt, and then use their responses to improve your business to target those needs.

10. LOVE THE JOURNEY

They say that happiness is 95% based on your own choices. If you are having a bad day, try to move your thoughts away from the negatives and instead focus on the positives. Imagine what it is going to feel like when your business makes it.

Remind yourself that the pain is temporary. Never let negative emotions influence you to make bad decisions. You don't want to make poor choices that seriously affect your success. Stay positive and keep motivated!

WHAT'S NEXT?

What you have just read are ten of the most important tips to get off on the right foot with your business. This advice will be vital to your success. Now, let's go into a little more detail and discuss how you can apply these tips to form a solid business plan.

WHICH PLAN WORKS FOR YOU?

CHAPTER 03

What follows are two plans designed to provide you with some clear and concise step-by-step direction for success. These are the two main business plans for the clothing industry. Look them over and decide which plan appeals to you. Then, put together a plan for yourself that works right for your situation.

PLAN "A"

While we will talk more about branding in future chapters, this will get you started.

1.   Brainstorm some ideas about your possible brand. These are ideas that represent your company, not ideas for the name of your business. For example, what do you want your brand to stand for? What are the most important characteristics you want your business to portray?

2.   After you have written down every random thought that surfaces, group related ideas, then work them into a brand name (or theme) that best describes what you are about.

3.   Repeat steps 1 and 2 a few times until you are happy with the results. Now your idea can be called a brand.

4.   Give your brand a strong presence, an identity. Carefully select words that accurately reflect the values behind your brand.

5.   Think of additional services and products that this brand could offer.

6.   Develop these ideas so that your brand becomes a collection of potential products.

7.   Inform people about your brand long before you begin to sell it.

8.   Develop a marketing plan for your product line.

9.   Begin to sell your products online.

10.   Develop your advertising to gain a larger following. Inform newspapers, radio, television, blogs, and social media about your brand.

11.   Begin to advertise your brand.

12.   Customers begin to buy your products and say that they will be back for more.

PLAN "A" (Continued)

13.   Find more ways to advertise your business.

14.   Regularly create fresh collections so that your brand doesn't become "old." You should do at least 9-11 drops a year (2-3 per season).

15.   Keep repeating step 5 to 13 until your brand is big enough to attract commercial retail businesses like Pacsun, and Zumiez to your products.

16.   Create linesheets and lookbooks that show what products you have and what they cost.

17.   Commercial retail businesses receive these linesheets and lookbooks and begin to buy your products (at wholesale prices, not retail pricing).

18.   Keep updating your website so that you establish an international customer base.

19.   Keep repeating the entire process until you have enough money to open up your own retail or chain of retail shops.

20.   Hire good management, sit back, relax, and watch the money come in.

PLAN "B"

14.　　Repeat steps 1 to 13 in Plan "A" as many times as necessary until you are ready to proceed.

15.　　Open up your own retail store or chain of retail shops and keep your products exclusive to your store.

16.　　Keep expanding with additional storefronts. Sit back, relax, and watch the money come in.

MAKE YOUR SUCCESS

These are a couple paths that many clothing lines travel, but these do not define the only way to success. It is essential to choose what will work best for you and for the growth of your business. Your business plan may have more or different steps than these. That's fine.

The more research and planning you do, the better developed your business plan will become. A business plan doesn't have to be super-complicated, but you do need some sort of guide for your business. If you don't have a clear vision of where you want your company to be in a year, then you will just be spending money and time with no real direction. Just make sure that you take action as soon as you find answers to your branding questions.

PLAN TO SUCCEED, OR PLAN TO FAIL

CHAPTER 04

Regardless of which plan you have chosen from the previous chapter, at least you have taken the first steps toward implementing a business plan. Whether you decided you prefer to build a primarily wholesale business, or whether you prefer the added responsibility of plan B – controlling all aspects of the customer experience yourself, it does not matter. Both options require a clear direction or plan to succeed. But how do you make sure that you are planning successfully?

SMART GOALS

One of the most well-known goal-setting methods in the business world is the word "**S.M.A.R.T.**" Smart goals are goals that are Specific, Measurable, Attainable, Relevant, and Time-bound.

Specific: Answer the five Ws about your business: who, what, where, when and why.

Measurable: You must have a standard with which to measure your progress and to tell when you have actually reached your goals.

It is also important to be able to measure the goals that you set. If you set targets and benchmarks and you reach them, then your goals become real and achievable and you will be inspired to do better next month. In the process, as you complete your goals and expand them, your goals and your business will continue to grow. If you don't measure your results, then you won't understand why you aren't succeeding. If you don't plan goals and measure the results of your efforts to reach those goals, then you will not know if you are successful or not, and you likely will not be successful.

Attainable: Ensure that your goals are realistic, that they can actually be achieved, and can be completed within your "when."

Always make sure that your goals are set within a realistic time frame. A sample realistic goal would be to sell 100 t-shirts within your first 3 months of operation. An unrealistic goal would be to say that you are going to get into a retail big box store in less than a month of starting your business. Believe me, if you set up goals that are mostly impossible to achieve, you are going to be very disappointed.

Relevant: Check that your goals are related to your brand and connected to your overall objective for your business.

Time-bound: There is always a time limit to your goals. Otherwise it is too easy to be always working and never achieving.

If you have trouble setting goals for yourself, use the following questions to determine what goals you should be setting.

1. In my first 3 months of operation, how many t-shirts do I want to sell?

2. Do I eventually want to sell my t-shirts to commercial retail businesses, or do I prefer to open up my own retail store to sell them myself?

3. Do I want my brand to stay small or go global?

4. How many blog posts or magazine articles do I want written about my brand?

This is what is meant when we talk about **SMART** goals, and these can be applied to any business scenario, as well as to other situations in your life.

Once you have some goals in mind, it is time to look at what you can do to set yourself up to reach those goals.

SET DAILY AND WEEKLY TASKS THAT CAN BE CHECKED OFF ONCE THEY HAVE BEEN COMPLETED

Now that you have your goals in mind and know that they are realistic and attainable, you must structure your daily life so that you are constantly working toward those goals until you achieve them. In order to do this, you will need to write down one of your goals and then break it down into the measurable steps necessary to reach that goal. For example, let's say you are ready to begin marketing your brand and want to have it advertised on three websites by the end of the week. You would write down something like this:

1.   Write up an article explaining my business and how unique my designs are in comparison to my competitors'.

2.   Research which websites/blogs are relevant to my brand and write down a list of those key sites.

3.   Contact each site about my brand, sending them the article I prepared, along with several high quality photos of the product(s).

4.   Follow up to answer questions and to encourage them to use my material on their site.

5.   Research more websites. Even if the first list was unsuccessful, you will eventually find those sites that see the value in your product.

Looking at the above steps, you can see that the goal of having your brand advertised on three websites by the end of the week is actually made up of five smaller sub-goals. When you look at a goal simply as a series of smaller activities, then you can measure how close you are to actually reaching it. Everything comes down to planning.

Now, when you look at the bigger goals you've been struggling with, you can break them down into a collection of smaller sub-goals that can be checked off as they are completed. I want you to start practicing this form of goal-setting by writing up a list of realistic goals you want to achieve by the end of each day, week, or month. Then, write up the steps necessary to achieve them. Each day, as you work toward your goals, you will be checking off the steps you have completed. At the end of the day, week, or month, you can look back and see exactly how much progress you have made.

DON'T OVER-PLAN

As important as planning is, it is also important not to plan so much that you plan your way to defeat. It is vital that you learn to recognize the moment when your plan is ready to be implemented. Otherwise, you can easily waste quality time trying to polish the perfect plan, when your time would be better spent implementing it.

As long as you follow the smaller steps that lead you toward your larger goals, you will be on the right track to success. Just keep in mind what are your goals and what steps are needed to reach them. Trust your research and planning and set your sights on the next step to be completed.

LOOK AROUND YOU; WHAT DO YOU SEE?

CHAPTER 05

After you've identified your goals and have taken a look at the steps you can take to reach those goals, the next thing you need to add to your arsenal is more research. Without research, you will have no idea what is going on around you. You will have holes and blind spots in your business that will become weaknesses over time. You can combat this problem by looking at six questions designed to further move your t-shirt business along the road to success.

1. WHO IS MY POTENTIAL CUSTOMER?

Actually, your first question should be, "Do I have a potential customer?" If you already have a potentially great idea, restrain yourself from speculation. Basically, don't assume you know what is good for other people. You want to eliminate as much guesswork as possible on your road to success, and this is just one step.

One of the biggest problems for companies these days is when they assume they know what people will like. They presume to know what people will want without researching and socially proofing the idea. Rushing and making bad decisions at this stage can lead to a lot of problems down the road. You don't want to be stuck with a garage full of products nobody wants. You also don't want to find yourself losing a lot of money from the get-go.

To avoid this scenario, test out of your idea to make sure there is a demand for it. Use a **Google Adwords** tool called the **Keyword Planner***. It doesn't take very long to create a **Gmail** account and fill in some basic information for an AdWords account to access it. Then, search for keywords that relate to your idea. Look to see if there is a high search volume; that will be a good indicator that your idea has a market.

Now that you know you do have a potential customer, what is your "niche" market? A niche market describes a highly specific customer base, a narrow target towards which you are aiming your product.

For example, if you made t-shirts with pictures of superheroes on them, they would sell to fans of superheroes. If you made t-shirts with pictures of fairies on them, they would sell best to people who love fairies. These can be considered niche markets, because they will only apply to a narrow subset of all customers who wear t-shirts. A niche is a specifically oriented market. You would not sell superhero shirts in the cooking marketplace. You may find people there who actually buy your shirts, but the chance of this happening is less likely than usual.

Most people go into the t-shirt business wanting to make shirts that appeal to everybody, then wonder why they have failed. The most successful clothing companies target specific niche markets, so they can dominate there. They specialize in reaching specific types of buyers with products tailored specifically for them.

It is essential to have a clear idea of who your customer is and why they would choose your brand, as opposed to the thousands of other t-shirt brands in the world. The best way to determine which niche markets you should target can be determined by the following questions:

1.   What hobbies and interests do my potential buyers have?
2.   What type of people do I want to wear my t-shirts? Children? Adults? Students? Athletes?
3.   Who would find my t-shirts most useful?

Once you have answered these questions, you have found your niche market. Just remember to make sure the niche population is large enough to support your product.

2. HAS MY IDEA BEEN USED BEFORE?

How many times have you come up with a great idea for an invention, only to find out that somebody has done it already? This is where research can really save your time and money. You don't want to spend a lot of time on something another person already has rights to. Do a detailed search of brand ideas similar to yours to see how close you are to them. If your idea is unique, then you are free and clear, but if your idea overlaps another person's you will need to get some legal help to see if you can create your idea without running into copyright restrictions.

3. IS MY BRAND NAME ALREADY IN USE?

Always check business and trademark registries to make sure that your unique brand name is not being currently used. You can look up trademarks on the US Patent and Trademark Offices website at **www.USPTO.gov***. Also make sure that the domain name for your brand/company is available. You can easily do a domain name search at any hosting website site like **www.HostGator.com***, **www.BlueHost. com***, or **www.Domain.com***. This is extremely important because your domain name will be the online platform customers go to when they want to learn more about your products (and hopefully buy them). This name in a very large sense represents everything you stand for.

4. WHAT EXACTLY IS MY BRAND ABOUT?

One of a business owner's greatest assets is his expertise on his products and services. You wouldn't sell boats if you knew nothing about boats. In the same way, you want your brand image to represent something you know a lot about. This means – you guessed it – more research. But don't consider it a waste of time; you are building a quality foundation for your life as well as for your business.

Do an extensive search on Google to make sure your brand name is not an offensive word in another language. The last thing you want is for your brand name to carry a negative meaning!

Case in point: Ford once made the costly mistake of marketing its Nova in Mexico. The sale was a complete bust. Why? In Spanish, "no va" basically means, "it doesn't go!" Don't be like Ford. Do your research!

5. WHAT DO OTHER PEOPLE THINK OF MY IDEA?

It is always important to run your ideas by other people (family and friends, for example), to make sure that the "cool" idea you have doesn't appear lame to others. The feedback these people give you could be a good indicator of what your potential customers will think. Would you purchase a product that comes across as lame and boring? Probably not.

It is also good to run your brand name itself across others to see how they react to it. Be willing to keep evolving your products and your brand name until you are confident in their potential. Once you are confident in them, it is time to launch your business.

Start validating your business in small and local venues on Facebook. Reach out to people you expect to be interested in the idea. Don't spam all your friends; you don't want to ruin your rapport with them, nor lose their friendship. Instead of mass messaging a bunch of random people, send a personalized message to a few individuals you think would be interested. Keep your message brief and informal. Gear your text toward their interests, interests you have found (from your extensive research) that will prove attractive to them. Use a short bulleted list of the features of your product. Ask your readers if this product is something they would actually buy? You don't just want to hear if it's cool or interesting; you want to know if they would actually purchase this product if you did make it.

6. WHAT OTHER BRANDS INSPIRE YOU?

Write down a list of the brands and companies that have inspired you. Read stories of their success, how they started, challenges that they faced and how they overcame them, as well as anything else that will help inspire you to pursue your goals.

Then write down the vision you have for your brand. By doing this it will help you know how you can stand out from the other brands out there.

CREATE MORE THAN JUST A BRAND

CHAPTER 06

When you think of the word "Nike", what comes to your mind first? That's right, the company's whole series of designs, and probably its swish logo as well. You might have also thought about the quality of their products and how much money people are willing to spend on their shoes. As you can see, with your business you are creating more than just a brand – you are creating an impact on your customers much bigger than just the sale of t-shirts.

Think about Nike again. Most people aren't buying their products just because they are like any other shoe. They are buying Nike's products because of the reputation the brand has built up over many years business. Nike's shoes may not always have the best quality in the world, but Nike's strong brand images have created a loyal customer base that will buy nothing but Nike's brand of products.

A BRAND IS A PERSONALITY

A strong brand has the ability to invoke the same emotions you would feel when interacting with a human being or an object in Nature. Yes, you are building an entity with its own personality. Your brand is not just the t-shirts you sell, but it is also represented by the people who sell them, the storefronts they are sold in, and even the people who answer the phones for your company. All of these make up the brand, so it is very important to ensure that your brand is represented consistently across the board. All areas of your business must work together as a single unit to contribute to the identity of your brand. Any weaknesses in your business will not only damage your bottom line but will hurt the brand image you have worked so hard to establish.

This chapter will help you determine the personality you want your brand to portray.

WHAT DOES MY BRAND STAND FOR?

Every successful brand has a story to tell. The story tells what you stand for. This standpoint will be unique; it is the one thing that separates your brand from your competitors. Perhaps you have an original idea that no other business has ever offered before, or maybe you can offer a guarantee that no other brand can. Whatever the case, build your brand about that one unique fact. Failure to clearly define your brand at this point may well lose you customers who could have been your most loyal backers.

The key is to be completely honest about what you can provide. For example, if your unique selling point is to offer a higher quality of clothing than a competitor, don't ever get caught selling a product of inferior quality! You don't want to ever send a message that contradicts your brand's values. That would only confuse – and ultimately lose you – your customers. Stay true to your word.

WHAT IS IN A NAME?

If you have a unique selling point and a strong brand name, then you can be assured of a degree of success. A brand name must be likable, easily remembered, and it absolutely must exhibit the qualities that your brand represents.

Be careful of choosing a name that limits what your brand can sell. For example, Nike uses only this short name since Nike Sneakers would restrict the brand to only

WHAT IS IN A NAME? (Continued)

selling sneakers. With the word Nike, the brand is able to market to a much broader audience and to include everything from shoes to clothing in its collection.

Therefore, it is wise to avoid using words such as "apparel" or "clothing" as part of your brand. As with the Nike example, the addition of an industry-descriptive word will restrict your brand's market potential if you ever decide to sell products outside of that industry.

KNOW WHAT YOU OFFER

Let's say you decide to sign up for a dating service. When you make your profile, you will take plenty of time, because you know you're selling yourself to a potential partner. You want to be sure the other person knows exactly what you stand for and has a clear understanding of why they should choose you over thousands of other potential candidates. The same applies for your business. Whenever anyone from your business represents it, you must make sure this spokesperson has a clear idea of exactly what your brand stands for.

Whether your brand is represented by a person, through social media, on a website, or even in a paid advertisement, you will only have one chance to make a strong first impression. You want that first contact with your brand to draw in the potential consumer.

It is important to be willing to spend all the time and effort necessary at this point. You have only a few seconds to convince the consumer to use your goods and services. You must be able to communicate what you stand for clearly enough for them to "get" your essence, without further elaboration. If your potential customers can not grasp the core of your brand in a couple seconds, they will simply look elsewhere.

Here are some additional questions to answer as you develop your business plan:

1.   How does my brand carry out its vision through my products?
2.   How can I develop a consistent brand-based theme or design that ties together all my products?
3.   What are three words I can use to describe my brand?
4.   What are two major selling points my brand offers that my competition does not?

KNOW WHAT YOU OFFER (Continued)

If you don't have any problems answering those questions, then you are on the right track. If you are encountering difficulty, don't panic. Just go back to the questions in the previous chapters and work through them until you are able to create a solid brand image and profile.

It's a great idea here to create a mood board. A mood board is basically a collage of items of existing products, items, people, and designs that relate to your brand. For example, if your brand is appealing to skateboarders, you could create a mood board of popular skateboard decks on the market right now, as well as pictures of skaters, and other products they love and wear.

Now that you have assembled a mood board, you can see the similarities of features that are shown across that industry. This will help you come up with ideas that relate to the same topic, but are tailored to your brand. It's great to make new mood boards every time you are working on a new collection of designs or products you plan on releasing.

HOW TO VISUALIZE YOUR BRAND

Once you have a strong brand profile, it is time to think of how you want to portray it to your potential customers. What the public will see comes down to four main factors: font style, images, the color palette, and your logo design. Each of these elements should complement the other. Any imbalance, and customers will attach laziness and unprofessionalism to your brand.

The image that represents your brand should also complement your brand profile. For example, a clothing line that produces nothing but lavish and high-end elegant apparel, such as Prada, is not going to mass produce $5 tank tops, because this goes directly against what the brand represents.

If you can create a strong and lasting visual impression, then you are well on the way to capturing a loyal fan base that will be your customers for life.

THE LAW COMES INTO PLAY

CHAPTER 07

Before you launch your t-shirt business, it is very important that you research the laws and legislation that apply to your industry. If legal issues are something you just don't understand or if you do not want to get involved in them, you must at least hire a professional to advise you before you start making critical business decisions.

If you fail to follow the laws that have been set in place to protect everyone in the t-shirt industry, as well as their customers, you risk major legal problems. The worst-case scenario is being sued; as a result you might even lose entire business. These laws exist to protect you, as much as to protect the other people associated with your industry. They stop other people from stealing your ideas, as well as preventing you from stealing theirs.

COPYRIGHT AND TRADEMARKS

A copyright gives the copyright holder the right to be credited for his or her work, to control who may adapt your work and release it in other media, and to determine who is allowed to financially benefit from it. A trademark is a form of intellectual property; it typically consists of a name, word, phrase, logo symbol, or may be a combination of these elements.

It is always advisable to register a copyright on your tee designs and also create a trademark to protect your brand and its profile. If you have the money to do both of these things, then do so immediately, but don't panic if you can't afford it right now. You don't need a copyright and a trademark in order to start a t-shirt business. When you are ready to protect your brand, one good place to start is **www.legalzoom.com** where you can purchase a trademark for your brand for around $400-600 (subject to change).

While the chances of someone stealing your idea before your business grows large enough for other people to notice it are relatively small, it is still important to protect the time and effort you have invested into cultivating your creative ideas. You can start by including a small "**TM**", ©, or "**R**" symbol beside your logo. As soon as you can afford it, apply for copyright and trademark protection

THE LEGALITIES OF INSPIRATION

When brainstorming creative ideas, it is always important to take into consideration where those ideas came from and how closely your ideas match what inspired you. Let's take a look at some common sources of inspiration and how we can avoid copyright and trademark violations.

PICTURES SOURCED FROM THE INTERNET

Probably the safest internet source for images is **www.creativecommons. org***, which displays pictures that are free to use without any copyright restrictions. There are several other ways to avoid copyright infractions. An image of a cat is considered a general image and lives in the public domain. However, a picture of the McDonald's logo is a brand-specific representation and is obviously heavily protected by both copyright and trademark law. Images that are specific and unique in nature are the most likely to be protected. Before you associate any image with your brand, check its status to avoid any potential conflicts with existing trademark and copyright holders.

QUOTES FROM PEOPLE

This one is fairly simple. Just credit – by name – the person who originated the quote.

USING CARTOON CHARACTERS

Never use famous cartoon characters without explicit permission. If you get caught selling t-shirts of Homer Simpson without permission, the penalty will be very severe. If you want to use a cartoon character in your design, draw one yourself or get a professional to design one for you.

If you really feel the need to use an existing cartoon character, you will need to negotiate permission with the copyright holder. Oh, and, prepare to pay royalties for the use of their image.

PARODY AND SATIRE

You are protected by the Right to Parody, which allows you to use famous people and characters in a satirical manner, in a parody, or in a caricature; just don't go too far. Avoid offensive, sexist, and racist material, which can easily get you into trouble.

POLITICIANS

You pretty much have free reign with images of politicians, flags, and national symbols. Just keep in mind that a photograph of a politician, prime minister or a president, may well be copyright protected.

PAPERWORK

It is essential you understand the paperwork behind legal and contractual agreements. I highly recommend employing a copyright lawyer or other legal professional to review and explain the terms and conditions of each legal agreement before you sign it.

TYPES OF BUSINESS STRUCTURES

There are several ways you can legally structure your business. We will explore which structure will best meet your business needs. Before you choose, you should take another look at **www.legalzoom.com***, which provides high-quality information about business structures and the legalities involved for each.

It is recommended that you start your business as a Limited Liability Company (LLC), because this protects you from liability, as the business owner, for any debts or liabilities the business many incur. Limited Liability Companies also require less paperwork and are more flexible than a Sole Proprietorship structure.

Unlike other business structures, your personal assets, including cars, houses, bank accounts, savings, and anything else of monetary value are safe from being seized if the business goes into debt. It costs $300-$600 to establish an LLC business structure. The cost is definitely worth the investment.

If you cannot afford an LLC structure, you should at least register yourself as a **DBA** (which means "Doing Business As"), since it costs a lot less than registering an LLC. DBA registration will allow you to open a bank account for the business, but provides no protection to your assets. Hopefully, this will only be a temporary measure, until your business develops to the point that you can afford LLC registration.

The main business structures are as follows:

1.   **SOLE PROPRIETORSHIP:** a business which legally has no separate existence apart from its owner. Income and losses are taxed on the individual's personal income tax return. Sole proprietorship is the simplest form of business structure, but is not considered a legal entity.

2.   **PARTNERSHIP:** a business in which two or more individuals manage and operate the business. Both owners are equally and personally liable for debts incurred by the business.

3.   **LIMITED LIABILITY COMPANY (LLC):** a corporate structure whereby the members of the company cannot be held personally responsible for the company's debts or liabilities.

4. **LIMITED LIABILITY PARTNERSHIP (LLP):** a partnership in which some or all partners (depending on jurisdiction) carry limited liability. This structure exhibits elements of both partnerships and corporations. In an LLP, one partner is not held responsible for another partner's misconduct or negligence.

5. **CORPORATION:** a large company or group of companies authorized to act as a single entity and recognized as such by law.

WHAT IT COSTS TO START A T-SHIRT BUSINESS

CHAPTER 08

Before you start up your t-shirt business, you must understand the costs involved. Typically, a t-shirt start-up will cost anywhere from $500, to upwards of $30,000. The costs involved depend on the your existing resources, the people or businesses that you know, and how much work is required to manufacture your products. What follows are a few examples of costs that may be involved for a start-up t-shirt business:

Print 6 designs, 4 tees each for 6 sizes	$864	144 shirts at $6 each
3-color ink per shirt	$252	$1.75 per shirt print
18 screens for color prints	$180	$10 each
144 Woven labels	$80	$0.55 each
144 printed inside sizing labels	$93.60	$0.65 each
144 bags	$20	$0.14 each
144 mailers	$30	$0.21 each
Sewing machine	$50	(prorate later)
Postage/shipping charges for everything sent to you	$75	$0.52 each
Setting up QuickBooks accounting: $12.95/ month)	$77.70	For 6 months
E-commerce website set-up (domain name, hosting, plugins, theme, SSL certification, photos, etc.)	$1,000	(varies)
TOTAL COST	**$2,772.30**	

At the very minimum, you should allocate $1,000 for your start-up. You could reduce costs by printing fewer tees, but you will only get out of the business what you put into the business.

HOW TO GET FUNDED

You don't necessarily need to take out a second mortgage on your house, apply for a credit card, or take out a loan with the bank to get started. Mortgages and credit cards become very expensive very quickly. In order to get a bank loan, you must first show that your business is making money, but how can you do that if the business has not even started running? The answer is to look outside of banks for funds to finance your business start-up. Take a look at the following ideas and see if any could work for you.

ASK YOUR FAMILY

When asking for money from your family, especially for something as risky as a business investment, it is very important that you take the conversation as seriously as you would with a bank manager. You are proposing a business plan to them, something that could be a valuable investment. You must convince your family that you are dedicated and serious about your venture. They must be confident that your business plan is sound. They also must believe you can give them a return on their investment. Just as you would pay interest on a bank loan, plan to pay back the principle of their investment, plus more.

And don't just make a verbal agreement. Ask them to sign a written agreement which states:

- How much, specifically, they will be investing
- When they will be completely paid back
- How much they will be paid in return
- A detailed schedule for repayment.

If you act like a serious professional, your family will treat you as a serious professional and may well offer you the investment money you need to get started.

PITCH TO YOUR FRIENDS

First ask friends who are already in business or working as professionals first if they would invest in your new business. If one friend cannot underwrite the entire cost, consider inviting several friends to contribute smaller amounts. Treat them as professionally as you would your family, including a similar written contractual agreement.

GET HELP FROM KICKSTARTER

www.Kickstarter.com* is a great potential resource for funding your business. This crowd sourcing website makes it possible for people to present unique business ideas and inventions to the general public. It provides a forum where individuals can donate anywhere from $5 to $2,000. In return, you offer them something, which could range from a thank-you letter to a signed tee. The idea is well worth looking into.

ENTER DESIGN COMPETITIONS

If you are confident in your skills and abilities as a designer or an artist, you should consider entering some of your work into a design competition. You can win cash prizes up to $20,000, which would definitely put you ahead both financially and in reputation. Some competitions can be unearthed at **www.Threadless.com*** and **www.Designbyhumans.com***.

FREELANCE WORK

Another way to capitalize on your skills as a successful designer, is to offer your skills as a freelancer. Some good sources for freelance work are:

- Google; search for "graphic design freelance work".
- Search on Craigslist under "Gigs" for small jobs.
- Sign on as a freelance designer with **www.Upwork.com***.

The money you bring in may not be huge, but over time these small jobs can contribute to your start-up savings. Then, when you have enough money, you can simply stop freelancing and focus instead on establishing your business.

TAP INTO SAVINGS

If you are currently employed, consider setting aside at least 10% of your income for your t-shirt business. If you earn $800 every week, and the cost to start your business is $2,000, you would set aside $80 per week. At this rate it would only take 25 weeks – just under six months – to reach your start-up goal. If you combine your weekly savings from your job with freelance work on the side, you could easily reach your investment target in 12 weeks or less.

SELL THOSE DUST TRAPS

Take a look in your garage, your closet, or around your house. If you find clothes you no longer wear, games you no longer play, or tools you no longer use, consider selling them online (at **www.eBay.com** or **Craigslist.org**). You could also have a garage sale. If you get lucky, who knows? You just might reach your investment target in a single weekend!

HOW TO DESIGN A TEE

CHAPTER 09

Another key to your success, is your ability to create stunning designs that people will want to buy. There are several factors to consider when designing a t-shirt, so let's take a look at them.

WHAT MAKES FOR AN AWESOME T-SHIRT DESIGN?

In the beginning of your business venture, it may take some trial-and-error to discover which designs work best and which designs don't work at all. What defines a good design? A good design can be defined as one that succeeds at communicating its intended message while being aesthetically pleasing to its intended audience. If you have the ability to make good designs right away, then great. If you're not so extraordinarily blessed, keep practicing until you get it right.

HOW DO YOU GET STARTED?

Once you know what you want your brand to stand for, the design process should be relatively simple. To get started, do image searches on the words that define your brand; use the results to stimulate inspiration for your own designs. As you start fleshing out sketches and design ideas, make multiple variations by shifting around the layout and by changing the colors; in this way you can start building a collection of original designs.

NAME YOUR DESIGNS BEFORE THEY ARE FINISHED

When you name your ideas, they become more grounded in reality. Then you can work from the designs themselves to create additional work based on different aspects of that name.

WHAT MAKES DIFFERENT DESIGNS COST DIFFERENTLY?

Without getting into the logistical details, think about the complexity of your design and list the costs you think will be involved to make it. Some designs may contain multiple layers or colors; this means that they would have to go through several printing processes before they are ready to sell. These costs add up rather quickly, so it is probably best to stick to simple ideas until your business grows a bit. When you can afford to spend money on more complex designs, you will be rewarding your customer base with a fresh, stepped-up product to enjoy.

WHAT DOES MY COLLECTION LOOK LIKE TOGETHER?

While creating different variants and types of design, always remember that your brand profile must be reflected there. When you put your designs together in a single collection, you want to see a common theme.

You want your brand characteristics to be easily picked out. You want your final product to represent what you stand for. You don't want your shirts to be so different from each other that the public is unable to recognize them as part of a single brand. Even something as small as a logo can be used to unify your collection.

WHAT DEFINES A COLLECTION?

At minimum, you should aim to have between 4 and 8 different designs, and you should plan to consistently add to this base as your brand expands and your business grows. Even if you have to start with fewer designs a distinguishable brand will lay the foundation for additions to your portfolio that will be immediately recognizable to your customers.

SO, DO I DRAW WITH CRAYONS, OR WHAT?

When you are first testing out different design possibilities, it matters little how you represent them. Even a sketch on a napkin can accurately portray your idea to friends and family. After settling on some design ideas however, it is time to start actually drawing them up in a professional manner.

There are two must have standard programs to use:

Adobe Illustrator*
Adobe Photoshop*

Both of these applications are used to digitize your designs and separate out the colors to make them ready for printing. If you lack access to either of these pieces of software, you can always search online for "free image editors" or even use **www.Pixlr.com***. If you aren't comfortable, you can always employ a graphic designer, but I'll will talk about that later.

If you will be screen printing your designs, these software programs can separate each color in the design for you. As well as it is very easy to resize your work and edit it.

CREATING THE BEST DESIGN

You should be using dimensions of at least 12 inches (width) and 16 inches (height) at a resolution of at least 300dpi (dots per inch). You can vary the size of the design, but make sure you stick with the 300dpi setting if you want to keep your designs in high-solution. Always remember that high-quality designs will set you apart from the crowd and ahead of your competition, and is vital when creating a strong brand profile.

FEEDBACK BEFORE YOU PRINT

Ask your friends and family for their opinion of your designs before you decide to go and print a hundred tees. If your designs are not up to par, and you receive negative feedback after you have printed, it will be a very expensive decision that you have made. You can also consider posting images on Facebook and Instagram to see what kind of response that you get, or think about submitting your designs to a t-shirt competition like threadless.com. You might actually win and have your business started for less than what you thought!

REVISION AND THE FINAL EDIT

Keep working on the cycle of design, feedback, and revision until you are 100% satisfied with the design that you have made. It is important that you take this very seriously as it is not only your designs that will suffer, but also the financial investment you will be putting into the business.

FINDING A SCREEN PRINTER

I recommend trying to a local screen printer, so that you can visit their facility, see the quality of their product samples, and ask them any questions. Going local also lets you receive your product on time and saves you money with shipping costs. If you can not find a local screen printer from a Google search, then you can try a site called **www.Taggler.com***. It's free to sign up. You post your shirt design with some details, and then screen printers will send you quotes on how much they would do the job for you. Remember don't just go with the cheapest quote. You want quality product so that you can sell it at a good price.

READY TO PRINT

For designs that you will be screen printing separate each color in the design into a separate layer. Each color layer is its own shape, which is then burned into screens which will be used during the transference of ink to your t-shirts. Save the file as a .PSD (Photoshop file), .AI (Illustrator file), or whatever file type the screen printer needs. When preparing a file for digital printing (DTG), the required file type is usually a JPEG (or JPG).

You can also provide your screen printer with a Pantone color guide of each color to be used in each design. This helps assure that the exact colors you want used in each design are the colors that get transferred to the final product. Besides color accuracy, one of the most important aspects of transferring a design to a t-shirt is size accuracy. Whenever preparing files for print, always make sure the dimensions of the file are the exact same dimensions of the design as you want it to appear on the final product.

HIRE A GRAPHIC DESIGNER

If you are not good at designing the t-shirts yourself, you can always hire a professional designer. A good place to find quality designers is to check out **Mintees.com***, **Coroflot.com***, and **Behance.net***. You can also consider making calls to your local designers or favorite indie designer and see how they might be able to help. Make sure that you spend some time researching each designer and looking at their previous work to judge if they will be able to make the right design for you, and have the potential to provide some high-quality work.

As an example, a professional designer can cost anywhere from $90 to $600 and potentially more, so make sure that you take these costs into consideration when writing up your business plan. You can also check out **Threadless.com*** and **Designbyhumans.com*** to see if you can buy designs from professional designers who may have not won a competition. That way, you will have a quality design that has already had some exposure.

THE FINAL DESIGN STEP

The final step in the initial design process is to create a "mock-up" of your designs. A "mock-up" is a digitally rendered image of what your t-shirt will look like when it is printed. You can find templates online to help you do this, and if you have hired a professional, ask them for mock-ups of the designs before they are finalized. The last thing that you want is a finalized design only to realize that it is not as good on fabric as it was on paper and have to start again!

PRODUCTION TIME

CHAPTER 10

Once you have finalized your designs and are ready to take them to the printers, there are still a few points to consider before you rush to the nearest manufacturer. If you want to create a brand that lasts, you must be highly involved in the details of the production process. After all, this is make-or-break time for your t-shirts. If any problems occur on the manufacturing end, you want to be there to address and resolve them as quickly as possible.

WHAT ARE THE COSTS?

Production is not the cheapest part of the process. It is important to carefully research the possible production companies and choose only those manufacturers who will be able to produce exactly what you require. Also you want to ensure that their price is not going to break the bank. Never choose the cheapest option; if you do, your business will suffer from compromises in quality. Money spent here is money well spent.

Most production companies at this stage will request 50% of the payment up front, and the other half after the work is completed. This can help your financial situation a lot as you can be raising the second half of the money while the tees are printing.

WHAT PRINTING TECHNIQUES ARE USED?

There are many different ways to have your t-shirts printed, but it is best to implement the techniques that will give you the most professional results. Decide which of the following printing methods will work best for you.

SCREEN PRINTING

Nearly all of the t-shirts that you see have been printed through this method. Screen printing uses a woven mesh to hold an ink-blocking stencil, of your design The attached stencil leaves open areas of mesh through which ink is transferred onto your shirt, resulting in a design which is both bold and crisp. Each printing color required a different stencil. The primary ink options include:

Plastisol Inks – The most commonly used inks for screen printing, made of PVC.

Metallic Inks – Shiny metal look, with a subtle, unfinished sheen.

Glitter Inks – Glittery specks all throughout. Similar to metallic inks.

Glow-In-The-Dark Inks – As the title implies, these inks glow in the dark; they come in a variety of glow characteristics.

High-Density Inks – Used to create an image that is raised up to 1/8 inch above the fabric's surface, giving you a slightly 3-dimensional print.

HEAT TRANSFER

Sometimes you want a different texture for your t-shirt design. In this case, a heat transfer is usually used. Heat transfer consists of a design on a specially printed paper which is transferred to the fabric using heat and pressure. Types of heat transfers can include:

Flock Transfers – These transfers have a smooth, fuzzy feel to them, somewhat similar to suede.

Foil Transfers – As the name suggests, these are shiny transfers made of foil.

OTHER METHODS

Dye Sublimation – A printing technique that allows printing of full-color images. This process results in a Tee with superior softness.

Embroidery – Needlework is used to apply a design in stitched strands of thread.

Patchwork – This method consists of machine-embroidering fabric cutouts on the shirt.

Stones, Glitter, or Studs – Adding these 3D shiny elements can be accomplished through a heat press or adhesives.

Direct To Garment – Special color printers are able to transfer images directly onto a shirt or other product.

WHICH METHOD IS MOST COMMON?

The standard method in the t-shirt printing industry is screen printing with plastisol inks.

WHAT PRINTER SHOULD I USE?

You should first select a printing method, so that when you present your designs to a manufacturer, you can ask if they are able to use that method to print your designs.

I recommend printing a sample of your first designs so you can see if the size and placement of your graphic is correct. You can do this by going online to

a DTG printer and submit one of your designs to be printed and mailed to you for around $16. Once you have your sample and get some good feedback, then place your order with a legit screen printer.

Before you approach a screen printing company, take a look at some of the company's previous work to gauge their standards and quality. Do they live up to your brand's quality level?

FINDING THE RIGHT BLANK TEE

Consider first who you expect to buy your shirts, and choose the most appropriate supplier accordingly. Looking at your closest competitors' choices of fit and style will help you decide what you should use. If your nearest competitors are using big loose crewnecks, then that's the type of fit you should use. If they're using tight V necks, then check into that option. Your competitors' customers represent your ideal customer so you want to give them something they are already accustomed to. For additional assistance, Google the following companies:

- Alternative Apparel
- Anvil
- American Apparel
- Alstyle
- Cotton Heritage
- Belle Canvas
- Hangs
- Gildan
- Next Level
- Tutlex

If you are still not sure about the t-shirts, you can always request some samples and take a feel for yourself. This is one reason I suggest doing your screen printing locally, so that you make a physical visit to see firsthand what they offer, try them on, and pick the ones you would like them to print. Once you are happy, put in a wholesale order for the t-shirts through the screen printer, a manufacturer, or online.

CUSTOM T-SHIRTS: CUT-N-SEW

All major t-shirt brands produce t-shirts via the cut-n-sew method, which basically means their t-shirts are produced from scratch according to the requirements their clients request. While this is more expensive than ordering bulk blanks, it gives you the advantage of total control over every step of the design process.

When looking for manufacturers that offer this method, consider a website like **www.Alibaba.com***, which provides a long list of manufacturers and suppliers that offer cut-n-sew shirts. Make sure that you always check the capabilities of each manufacturer, such as minimum and maximum order quantities, cost per tee, and so on. It might be a good idea to order a sample first before you decide to order 1,000 tees. Considering that each t-shirt may cost around $3 to produce, it can be an expensive decision if design or errors in capability are not caught quickly.

SIZES

Take a look at your customer base so that you can determine the size range of the t-shirts you should offer them. You are probably not going to be printing XXL size shirts for infants or XXS tees to adults. In addition, when you do determine the size range of your customer base, you do not need to print every single size within that range. Instead, look at printing only S, M, L, XL and maybe XXL. Most of your customers will fall within this range, and you can always order additional sizes upon request, should you need them. There is no point in ordering 50 XXS tees if you don't have a customer base that will be wearing them.

Look into getting sizing label stickers so it's easier to manage inventory when all your shirts are packaged and ready to go. Simply stick a size label sticker on the folded shirt.

WHAT IS IN A LABEL?

Labeling your shirts maximizes every opportunity to show off your logo. You should also aim to instruct your customers in correctly caring for the t-shirts they have bought from you. Take a look at the tag inside one of your own t-shirts; it should give you a clear idea of basic care instructions. Get the fabric details from the supplier or manufacturer, along with basic care instructions and include these in your custom designed logo-emblazoned tags.

Hang tags are another great way to show off your logo and impress your customers. You can also have a hem tag of your logo sewn onto your shirts.

Here are a few places you can order labels:

- CBF Labels / **www.cbflabels.com***
- Barrel Maker / **www.barrelmakerprinting.com***
- Clothing Labels4U / **www.clothinglabels4u.com***
- GotPrint / **www.gotprint.net*** Great for business cards, hang tags & flyers.

KEEP YOUR EYE ON PRODUCTION

Keep in touch with the manufacturer as often as possible throughout the ordering and printing process. Request photo updates throughout the process to ensure that the designs are being printed just as you have requested. Have them send the tracking numbers when the product is about to be shipped to you.

WHAT'S IN A PACKAGE?

The image on your t-shirts is not the only aspect of design worth considerable time and effort. What you package your tees into matters just as much. A customer may love your designs, but be turned off by cheap or unprofessional packaging, causing you to lose their business. My best advice is to look at what your closest competition is doing and match or better their packaging quality. Buy a shirt on sale from your closest competitor and see how they ship it to you. What you receive should determine the minimum quality level for your packaging.

The most common types of packaging are:
*   Plastic mailers
*   Tyvek mailers
*   Corrugated boxes

Even if you can only afford the cheapest packaging option when you start, you should include in your business plan a goal to pay for a higher-quality packaging as soon as you can afford it. At bare minimum, your tees should be packaged in a plastic poly bag. You can find a host of poly bags or tyvek mailers on **www.uline.com*** and **www.usps.com***.

When you can afford a better option, you should consider adding one of the following packaging options to your budget:
*   Colored or metallic poly mailer
*   Poly mailer with printed design or a logo sticker on it
*   Corrugated box mailer with your logo on it
*   Plastic box or mailing tube with logo sticker
*   Tin can or other custom shape

A good source of inspiration is to take a look at your favorite designers. Here are a few ideas for unique add-ins:
*   Die-cut custom-shaped hang tags
*   Stickers or posters that match t-shirt designs
*   Knick-knacks relevant to your brand
*   Collectible cards or a booklet
*   Coupons for future orders

YOUR CUSTOMERS DON'T WANT CHEAP

Your customers not only want a high-quality design with thought put into the packaging, but they also want you to oversee the production of the products they are buying. Don't cut corners. Definitely avoid setting yourself up as a fulfillment or "print-on-demand" business, where you print something only when it has been ordered.

Print on demand is extremely expensive, because you are not able to capture the discounts of bulk-printing. A bulk screen-printed tee may cost only $8 per shirt to produce, compared to a once-off print-on-demand tee at $28. That is a massive $20 that you could have used as profit instead of adding it into your printing costs!

It can also include longer production time than your customer are willing to wait. You can easily rack up multiple order cancellations and negative reviews, if your delivery time exceeds their patience. In the current market, speed of delivery is everything.

I also suggest minimizing your use of a fulfillment service because you cannot verify product quality, since the shirt never touches your hands. Your customers may receive a t-shirt with a crooked graphic on it and you would never know. At least you'll only know if they share their dissatisfaction online for the world to see!

Another disadvantage of using 3rd party fulfillment sites is that they can't add your finishing touches of hang tags, stickers, thank you messages, or woven labels. These little things are the indicators of high quality service that a lot of customers have come to expect.

SET UP SHOP

CHAPTER 11

Now that you have started to print your shirts, you need to ensure that you have somewhere to sell them! Let's start this chapter off with the basics of designing a website for a business where you will be able to sell your t-shirts.

WHAT MAKES A GOOD WEBSITE?

When choosing the products to sell on your website, it is vital that you include only your highest quality items. This way, you can rest assured that you are providing your customers with a delightful experience starting with the quality of your designs, and extending all the way down to the actual layout of your website.

The objective of your website: you want to make a great first impression. Since you have already determined your target market, your website design should reflect the values and interests of your customers. Your site will include a way for customers to pay you and will provide a straightforward ordering structure. Customers should be able to easily navigate your website, find what they are looking for, and then purchase their selections without any hassle.

Lets take a look at the "must-haves" for your e-commerce website.

EASE OF NAVIGATION

The goal of an e-commerce site is for the customer to leave with a purchase, so the design of your navigation tools should reflect that goal. It should be extremely easy to go from the home page to the product selection page and ultimately to the cart/checkout page.

You will need two separate navigation areas on your website. One will serve as the primary navigation page and the other as a secondary shop navigator to sort through product categories. The main navigation section is best positioned horizontally across the top of the site. In the main navigation section, it's important to include Home, Shop, About, Cart, FAQ and Contact clickables.

In the shop navigation structure, you will include all of your product categories, including categories for New Products and On Sale. Once your website is built, test the ease of use by asking a friend to attempt a purchase.

STUNNING PRODUCT IMAGES

Set forth your product in its best light, literally as well as figuratively. A great product image can turn lookers into buyers and will be one of the keys to the success of your online store.

Low-quality product images from the start will destroy any chance you had of people buying from your shop. Take high-quality photos of your t-shirts and enhance them using photo-editing software to achieve the best possible representation of your product. If you can't do this yourself with a DSLR camera, hire someone to help you. Look online at **behance.net***, or create a Craigslist post under the gigs category.

If you want your photos to include models, have your friends stand in for you or hire models from **ModelMayhem.com***. Just make sure the models you use clearly represent the customer demographic you expect to buy your shirts. For example, if your company is a fitness brand then make sure you have models that appear in excellent physical shape.

Each product image should be at least 600 pixels wide, big enough for potential buyers to enlarge to see the details on their computer screen. Two to three alternate images of the product should also be included to give a good sense of what the product will look like in person. Include a front view, a side view, and a back view. List the size of the product the model is wearing and the height of the model so that viewers can get a better idea of its fit, and how it will look on them.

LOTS OF INFORMATION

Each product should include detailed written information. This detail can make or break a sale. Second only to the product image, this is one of the most important ways to maximize customer satisfaction and minimize merchandise returns.

Describe everything from the obvious to the tiniest detail of its construction. Be sure to include what the t-shirt is made of, the printing method or application used, and the colors of the t-shirt. Your product description should be short; up to three sentences should be sufficient. Be sure to list information that will give customers a good idea of what they are buying. You may wish to append a short, funny, or intriguing sentence or two about the product to extend your brand's personality and further convince a potential customer to make a purchase.

SIZES

Since your shop is online, visitors don't get to try your products on before buying them. If a customer orders a size that ends up being too loose or too tight this will result in a return. To maximize customer satisfaction and minimize returns, display a sizing chart on your site that lets your visitors know the precise measurements of each shirt size you offer.

The best place for your sizing chart to appear is on the individual product page for each item. There should be some type of link to a pop-up sizing chart, or a small image of the sizing chart that can be easily enlarged.

Rather than measuring each t-shirt size yourself, refer to the sizing chart already provided by the brand of t-shirt blanks you will be using. If your tees will be made from scratch, you'll already have the measurements, because you provided them to the manufacturer as part of your specifications.

In addition to a sizing chart, if your t-shirts don't fit true to size, be sure to point this out as part of your product description.

SECURITY AND PROTECTION

Even though we live in a day and age in which many people are comfortable with trusting personal information to the Internet, some are still concerned about online safety. You want to assure potential customers that your website is safe and trustworthy so they are more likely to make a purchase.

The best way to make sure your site is safe is to choose a shopping cart platform that processes payments securely. Almost every shopping cart platform out there already does this, so you won't have to worry too much. However, your visitors need explicit assurance before they buy. To inform your visitors about your site's security, simply display the platform's security seals prominently in your shopping cart area.

The most commonly used merchant service is **PayPal***. PayPal is free to sign up for and they process all credit card payments for a small fee. Then you can easily transfer the money you received from PayPal into your bank account. Your online shop will be verified by PayPal, which secures their information using **VeriSign Identity Protection**. If you choose to use PayPal, you should display the Paypal Verified seal and the VeriSign Identity Protection seal on your shop to show that all transactions are secure.

Include information about your site's security in a sentence or two on your FAQ page. For example, the answer to a question such as *"How secure is your shop?"*, would be: *"This store uses PayPal for all transactions. PayPal automatically encrypts your confidential information in transit from your computer to ours using Secure Socket Layer protocol (SSL) with an encryption key length of 128-bits (the highest level commercially available)."*

If your website already provides standard security features (**SSL protocol**, **VeriSign**, and/or **McAffee Identity Protection**), your shop should already be secure. It is up to you to let your visitors know about this protection, so they can feel safe when providing their credit card information on your site.

METHODS OF PAYMENT

The payment options you accept should consist of credit/debit cards and Paypal. If you want, you can include **Amazon Payments** or **Google Checkout** as an option, but only if it is already one of the default options for your e-commerce platform. Other payment options, such as checks or money orders, are not worth the hassle and risk they invariably incur.

The problem with checks and money orders is that checks can bounce, and either method can get lost en route to you. The vast majority of people who shop online will have either a debit/credit card or a Paypal account. Don't worry about the miniscule percentage of sales you might be missing out on by not allowing check or money-order payments.

In summary:

• Create your online shop on an e-commerce platform that accepts **credit/debit cards** and **Paypal**.

• Highlight the payment options you accept on your shopping cart page, and be sure to display the logos of the four major credit card providers: **VISA, MasterCard, American Express,** and **Discover**.

• Clearly state, both in your **FAQs** section and on your check-out page, the security procedures that are in place to protect your customers.

INFORMATION ON SHIPPING AND RETURNS

It's important to let potential customers know early on how much it will cost to have their order shipped to them and how long it will take to receive the products they ordered. If you don't indicate shipping costs in advance, you may end up with an overload of abandoned shopping carts. Abandoned carts indicate the customer added products to a cart but never completed the purchase. One possibility is that the customers were scared off by unexpected shipping and handling charges.

You should factor in how much it will cost you to ship products to your customers when deciding how much to charge for shipping. You should also check the website of your shipping carrier for estimated delivery times of each shipping

INFORMATION ON SHIPPING AND RETURNS (Continued)

method you plan on offering.

It's best to offer more than one shipping option, such as Standard and Express shipping. When first starting out, it simplifies matters to charge a flat shipping rate of $5 or $6 per item.

You should include your shipping information on the FAQ page and on a separate "Shipping and Returns" page. Details about how to process a return are essential, especially if you hope to attract repeat customers.

As for your product return and exchange requirements, decide on a time frame in which returns will be accepted and what condition the merchandise must be in to qualify. Indicate whether or not you will pay the shipping costs for returns and exchanges. And of course, follow through with processing all returns and exchanges in the manner you stated on your site.

FREQUENTLY ASKED QUESTIONS

Whenever you have questions about buying a product online, you take a look at the **FAQs** (Frequently Asked Questions) page. When creating a FAQ page, you should aim to answer all of the questions you think your customers may have including answers to questions your customers have asked in the past.

Look at the FAQs section of a competing brand's website and base your questions on theirs. Here are some questions to start off with:

- Is checkout secure and safe?
- Do you have sizing information?
- Which payment methods do you accept?
- How can I track my order?
- When will my order be shipped?
- Do you ship outside of the U.S.?
- What if the item doesn't fit?

These are some questions customers will consider asking either before they purchase or after they've purchased, so a FAQ page provides immediate answers to common and basic questions.

WHAT MAKES FOR GOOD WEB DESIGN?

Research has stated that when a customer lands on your website, you have five seconds to grab their attention before they take off for another site. You could easily lose business if you haven't put time and effort into designing a website that conveys simplicity, maintains customer interest, and encourages the customer to buy from you.

Good website design should match your brand profile. As we have discussed throughout this book, your collection should have a unifying element which pulls it all together. If you have a design collection that is all green, for example, you are not going to make a website dominated by the color orange. Your website is a part of your collection and serves as the main face of your brand's visual identity.

Choose a single font to use throughout your website. A standard choice for online business sites is the font **Helvetica**. The font color should be black, white or grey, depending on the background color. Grey text on a white background can be very difficult to read, for example; black would be a more legible option. Keep your page elements to a maximum of three colors that complement or match the color scheme of your brand's logo design.

WHAT TYPE OF E-COMMERCE PLATFORM SHOULD I USE?

Since there is a wide variety of e-commerce platforms on the market today, it can sometimes be difficult to determine which is the best and which will adequately fulfill your requirements.

Putting together a website all on your own can be extremely tough, especially if this is something you have never done before. Since your website will be the face of your business, your virtual shop front, it is valuable to pay a professional to create a high-quality website for you. This service can cost anywhere from $500 to $3,000. However, if you don't think your budget can support this amount of money, you can always consider doing an online search for free website templates or set up a store on one of the sites below. The following platforms are easy to use, and while they may not incorporate all the design ideas you have in mind, all you really need to do is sign up and go live, then upload your logo, some product photos, and your product descriptions and you're in business.

Shopify*

Pricing begins at $29/month in addition to the 2% that Shopify takes per transaction. Recently, Shopify unveiled "Shopify Payments" as their own payment gateway. This means you don't need to use an external payment gateway (which usually tacks on another 2.9% credit card fee). Shopify provides a genuine, robust shopping cart system. No other website builder is close. But it's an important thing to know who Shopify is for.

Cost: $9.99-$29.99/mo
Difficulty: Easy
Features: Intermediate-Advanced

Big Cartel*

This is a well-designed, simple-to-use e-commerce builder that will work well for small stores. Where its competitors often overwhelm with features and settings, Big Cartel takes the opposite approach, providing the basics wrapped in a product that's actually enjoyable to use.

Cost: $9.99-$29.99/mo
Difficulty: Easy
Features: Beginner

BigCommerce*

Very similar to Shopify in terms of core features, but this platform tends to favor already established merchants. BigCommerce has great support and a wonderful platform.

Cost: $9.99-$29.99/mo
Difficulty: Moderate
Features: Intermediated

Core Commerce*

Core Commerce's sign up process facilitates the easy setup of your store structure. Account creation is streamlined, and the Setup Wizard provides quick introductory access to some design options, shipping tools, and other goodies. You can create your first few products here (albeit with limited settings compared to the full dashboard) and choose which payment methods should be accepted.

Cost: $9.99-$29.99/mo
Difficulty: Moderate
Features: Advanced

Wordpress/Woo Commerce*

You've probably heard of Wordpress before. It's one of the most popular content management systems on the internet. Content Management Systems, or CMS's are a suite of programs that help you structure your website. You can think of them as a step above website builders in both complexity and power. They usually require some technical understanding to use. Once you have the Wordpress site setup you will need to install the Woo Commerce plugin to sell products on the site, and the theme needs to be compatible.

Cost: Free to setup, but themes costs $50+

Difficulty: Moderate

Features: Intermediate-Advanced

WRITE A BLOG

Blogging has become a big thing in social media. Individuals from all walks of life and all sorts of businesses blog in order to maximize the scope of their audience in the online world. It has become standard practice these days for designers and small to large fashion brands to blog. It could be a smart idea to join the crowd and start blogging. The three largest blogging platfroms are **Wordpress.org***, **Blogger.com***, and **Tumblr.com***.

If you don't feel capable of blogging, you can always incorporate a "**Latest Updates**" section into your website. This will allow your customers to click on – and have a look at – the latest news and upcoming events that pertain to your business.

It would still be a wise decision to start learning about blogging, and at least write one blog post each week. There are many advantages:

•   You can build a personal connection with your customers.
•   With a personal connection, your customers will be building a personal relationship with your brand.
•   It's a fun way to show your customers your funny side or connect to them via your witty personality.
•   It will encourage repeat business.
    – Every time you post a blog, people who follow your site will be reminded of you, keeping your name before them and enhancing name recognition.
    – If people enjoy reading your blogs, then they will be more likely to buy again from you, just to encourage and support you (there's the importance of that personal connection).
    – You can put a personal face to the characteristics of your brand; your customers begin to develop loyalty to you because they see in you the characteristics that they value in your brand.

A MARKETER'S DREAM

CHAPTER 12

A successful marketing strategy is one that exposes people to your brand within a very short time. It also holds their attention powerfully enough that they keep coming back for more. Marketing is an aspect of business where the most money should be spent after the design and production phases are complete. Not all marketing is expensive. There are many ways to market your brand, and some are even free!

USING ONLINE ADVERTISEMENTS TO PROMOTE YOUR WEBSITE

The best part of online advertising is that from the moment customers are drawn in by your ad, they are literally a single click away from purchasing your products. If you are smart with your ad placement, you can hope to see at least some (or maybe a lot of) customers directed to your website and to view your design collection. By "smart" I mean you display your ads in places where a lot of people are exposed to it, that is, in high traffic locations.

You can contact other websites and blogs to promote and advertise your products. It is generally considered that at least 800 visitors to a website a day are websites that you should be advertising on.

You should expect to pay between $100 and $250 in order to see decent results from an advertising campaign.

COST-PER-CLICK
GOOGLE ADWORDS

This marketing model is an excellent tool for those with a little extra money in their marketing budget. The reason it costs a little extra is because you place your advertisement on a website, but you only pay the website owner if and when somebody clicks on your ad. The good thing is that if nobody clicks on your advertisement, you are advertising for free. But if this marketing campaign suddenly becomes extremely successful, you could quickly be out of pocket several thousand dollars in per-click charges.

The best **CPC** (cost-per-click) provider is probably **Google AdWords***. It is worth the time and effort to check out for yourself exactly how it works and what it costs.

FACEBOOK IS A POWERFUL TOOL

As soon as you are ready to start promoting your brand, in addition to a website, you should also create social media accounts on both Facebook and Twitter (and possibly Instagram, as well). This will give you access to over 7 billion potential customers you probably would not have connected with otherwise. Be careful to make your social media profile match your design theme, and frequently update the information on these accounts.

You can link your business's Facebook and Twitter profiles to your website, meaning that your customers can "like" your page, as well as receive live updates to your latest news and sales in the palm of their hands. The "like" button is a very powerful tool if one of your customers likes your page, and one of their friends likes the page too, then one of their friends likes it, and so on. As you can see, theoretically, a single "like" has the potential to filter through the pages of multiple networks of friends, potentially reaching hundreds of new and potential customers!

Using a little money from your marketing budget, you can buy Low Cost Likes, to drive traffic to your website store and increase sales. I suggest first setting up an ad campaign to promote your Facebook page. The objective is to get 1,000 likes in less than 48 hours. Create a budget of $5.00 for 2 days, and run the ad in other countries for low cost likes of $0.01. Reach out to counties like India, Mexico, and the Philippines. If you run the ad in the United States you won't get that many likes, simply because it costs more to advertise your page in the United States. The purpose is initially to receive enough likes to social-proof your company and show that real people from around the world like your business. Once you have done that, then create an ad to drive traffic to your website. Make sure you use eye catching photos to get people to click and go to your website.

HOT OFF THE PRESS

Newspapers and editors love to write about things that generate hype, and this kind of hype is created for free! Think about what you can write to the newspapers, bloggers, and article websites that will catch their attention enough that they want to write about you and your brand. Just remember though, that these businesses receive hundreds, if not thousands, of press requests every day and week, so make sure you have a catchy title in your subject line, and keep your letter or message short and to the point.

Write only about what makes your brand (or you as representative of your brand) unique. Avoid information irrelevant to your brand's image. It's a good idea to create a press release page on your website with high res photos and a shareable write-up of your brand.

Send out bulk emails in the morning between 7:00am and 9:00am. If you send messages after 5:00pm, it will be buried in the bottom of the inbox by morning, when people check their emails. When you are working globally, you'll want to target separate releases to accommodate major differences in time zones.

Here's a sample email, targeting news outlets:

> *Hey (**name**), this is (**your name**) founder of (**your brand**), I want to share with you our story. I noticed that on your site you have been covering a lot of up-and-coming brands. I think (**company they work at**) readers would appreciate knowing about our new products. I recently released a collection of t-shirts and I think you'd find them interesting to share.*
>
> *We could drive some traffic and shares to it. My brand's website provides a press kit, complete with press releases and high res images I think you'd like.*
>
> *Here's the link: **http://www.yourbrand.com/pressrelease***
>
> *Let me know your thoughts,*
> *Thanks!*

NEWSLETTERS

I recommend you offer a newsletter to your visitors and customers. For the sake of those who sign up to receive it, discipline yourself to produce and distribute a newsletter each week if possible. If this is too much, at least commit yourself to posting once a month. Follow all the rules of design unification we have already discussed, and keep your articles relevant to your brand and products. When you mention your products, always include how they will benefit your customers. Building a strong readership to your newsletter (just like writing your blog), can create a loyal customer base built on repeat business. This can be your key to financial success!

SEO (SEARCH ENGINE OPTIMIZATION)

SEO, or Search Engine Optimization, consists of placing keywords or phrases strategically to cause your website to appear on the first page of Google's search results. This is a complex topic, but there is only room here to provide a brief description so you can at least grasp the basics of SEO.

Let's say that somebody went to Google to learn how to grow roses. What will she enter into the Google search field? The most likely phrases are "how to grow roses", or "rose growing guide". Google displays websites based on the most relevant search terms used. If your website contained the words "how to grow roses", then you would be ranked higher in the search results than a website that contained the words "planting roses". One warning though: overuse of certain keywords in your website in order to manipulate your ranking in Google's search results, could result in penalties from Google.

Another important thing to consider is if your website contains too many keywords and phrases. This overabundance might confuse Google into thinking your website is not relevant to the search terms. Always keep information on your website relevant. Avoid publishing irrelevant pieces of information; they may damage your visibility and drop you below the top page of search results. This, in turn, will affect how many customers navigate to your website based Google's search results.

KEEP UP WITH SOCIAL MEDIA

Keeping up with all your social media channels can be difficult. While you want to maintain a good presence on each of your media outlets, the challenge is to keep up with them.

The primary social media platforms to engage are **Facebook**, **Twitter**, **Instagram**, and **Pinterest**. You may also want to consider starting a **Youtube** channel for your future video advertising.

Design your social media platforms to reflect your brand and keep your user name consistent across them. Employ similar colors, fonts, and graphics across all communication media.

Once you have created these pages, look for ways to manage them together. Signing into each account every day can be a nightmare. I suggest you sign up to a social media management service like **HootSuite.com***. This application is free and will add likes to your Facebook and Twitter accounts. You will be able to mange, read, respond, and interact with people who follow you. The best part: you can schedule all your posts for advance release. Just pick one day a week to sign in and schedule all your posts for that week and you're done. Then you can focus on other important business tasks for the rest of the week.

HOW TO PRICE YOUR T-SHIRTS

In addition to your brand profile and efforts to marketing, another factor to consider is your t-shirt pricing. Not only does price affect how much money you will actually earn per shirt sold, it can also have an impact on how your customers perceive your brand. Setting your prices too low will either make you a lot of money, or cause your customers to perceive your brand as "cheap" and not worth their investment. On the other hand, if you set your prices too high your customers will either view your brand as a luxury item that they want desperately (making you even more money at a higher profit margin), or the price may turn customers away because it is too expensive for them to afford.

The best option is to stick somewhere in between the two extremes. $16 to $24 is considered the "unofficial" acceptable price range for the majority of t-shirt brands out there. This range will set your profit margins at an acceptable level for your customers, but will provide you enough profit to be able to maneuver around the competition of the industry. A moderate price range will allow you to make smaller orders (at higher production costs) and still make a healthy profit.

The next level up is the $25 to $32 price range. This is where many streetwear labels set their prices. Finally, all shirts above the $32 range tend to be considered luxury items, or brands with celebrity endorsements. The ordinary consumer at this level will pay almost anything to wear the same clothing as their favorite celebs.

The price ranges we just discussed are normally what you would sell your tees for, direct to your customer. However, if you decide to sell your shirts to retailers, your profit margin per tee becomes considerably lower. When you sell to retailers, you are in essence sharing your profit with the retailer The only upside to this is that retailers are able to give your brand a greater marketing push, so in the long run you may well end up making more money than by selling the tees yourself.

HOW TO PRICE YOUR T-SHIRTS (Continued)

Here are some examples of what retailers might pay for your shirts, depending on the retail price range you sell them for:

If your wholesale price is:	Your retail price should be:
$5 to $7.50	$10 to $15
$8 to $12	$16 to $24
$12.50 to $15	$25 to $30
$15.50 to $30	$31 to $60

Here are the equations that should guide your pricing:

Production Cost x 2 = Wholesale Price

Wholesale Price x 2 = Retail Price

If a tee cost you $4 to make, you would apply an $8 wholesale price to it, with a $16 retail price. Keep in mind though, that these prices are guidelines and many businesses will set their own prices. Some will command much lower prices or require higher margins, which affect both the wholesale and retail prices. For you, focus for now on always offering competitive pricing.

UP-SELL FOR MORE PROFIT

Professional salespeople are able to make money because they have mastered the art of up-selling. Up-selling is when a customer is in the process of making a purchase and you offer them additional products or services in hopes that they will accept and spend just a little more money. More money spent equals higher revenue, and higher revenue means higher profit, so you have good reason to learn this art and employ it correctly.

The best tactic to use when up-selling, is to offer the customer something for the same price or less than what they are currently spending. For example, if a customer buys two tees, offer them a third shirt for 40% off. You may make less profit on the third shirt than you would by selling it on its own, but it is better to sell right now at a discount than to wait and perhaps not be able to sell it at all. You have nothing really to lose and you have the chance to increase customer loyalty to boot.

Another powerful up-selling strategy is to offer the customer something inexpensive in addition to their current purchase. Most customers will not mind adding another couple bucks to their cart. For example, have you noticed in supermarkets that they position the candy bars and sodas near the checkout counter? Most people will pick one up when they are paying for their goods because they don't mind spending an extra two or three dollars for a candy bar when they are already spending much more money.

If even four out of ten customers picked up a candy bar, that makes for 40% more customers who are spending extra in the store. The profit margin may be very small on a candy bar, but if you consider that at least 1,000 people a day visit a busy supermarket, 40% would make for an extra 400 candy bars sold each day! That's, an additional 2,800 candy bars sold each week and more than 12,000 extra candy bars sold every month! When you look at it that way, you will understand just how much additional money your business can make through the power of up-selling.

Think about what additional lower-priced items you could add to your t-shirt business in order to up-sell your customers to gain greater revenue and profits.

LOOKBOOKS - MARKET SUCCESS

We have all seen fashion-wear and clothing in catalogs. They can be quite boring, right? That's why I'm advising you to steer clear of them and instead use lookbooks. A lookbook is simply a set of photographs of your designs that you release every quarter or season. They usually show models wearing your clothes, depicted in real-life situations, or posed in an artistic manner.

Imagine how elegant and sophisticated clothing looks in a fashion magazine. The images evoke emotional responses and tell a story through strong visual language and storytelling. This is what you want to achieve, a strong visual product that adds a background depth to your product.

Here are some tips that may help you develop a great lookbook:

1.   Look at what your competition has done. Review the lookbooks of other successful t-shirt businesses. Save some of the images from their lookbooks so you can reference them later when working with a photographer.

If you are selling t-shirts in a niche market and there are no other brands with lookbooks to copy from your niche, you should think twice about releasing one yourself. Remember that niche markets are small; your audience may be quite limited. It may not make sense to spend money on a lookbook if your niche market will not turn it into profits.

2.   Spend enough money to hire a skilled professional photographer. You will want high-quality, sharp, crisp photographs so don't settle for less than professional quality. Any photographer you use should be using a DSLR camera, the industry standard for high-quality shots.

Photographers aren't cheap, so choose carefully. You want the one you hire to have a good reputation and be able to show you previous work that matches or exceeds the type of work you are looking for.

Show your prospective photographer your collection of images drawn from your competitors' lookbooks. This will give the photographer an idea of what you are looking for and will provide a starting place for your collaboration.

LOOKBOOKS - MARKET SUCCESS (Continued)

3.   Choose settings that are different from the competition. You want your photographs to stand out from the crowd, so avoid cliché settings of beaches and parks. Instead, think of something unique that ties in with and supports your brand.

4.   Add depth to the shot by incorporating props into the foreground and background. This will render your photographs much more eye catching. Consciously plan every detail in your shots. Shoes, pants, backpacks, and jewelry should have unique character that will hold the eye of the beholder and enhance the values of your brand.

5.   If you can't afford professional models, consider asking family or friends to model for you. Just make sure they look like the demographic you are marketing to.

6.   Take more than one picture of the setting. This way your work won't go to waste if one of your photographs is ruined by a passing bird or stray person in the background. Consider using burst photography, where 10-30 photographs can be taken in a few seconds.

7.   Don't overuse your photos. Choose only your best shots. If you don't have enough high-quality shots at the end of the day, then consider either reshooting, or including fewer photos in your lookbook. Don't ever cut corners when it comes to visual quality.

8.   Enhance your images in Adobe Photoshop or another professional image editing application to ensure that both your brand and your shots are professional and up to the highest standard. A lot of photographers offer this service when you hire them, so make sure to ask about it.

9.   Release your lookbook on your website, social media profiles, blogs, and anywhere else you are planning to market and advertise your brand.

PRODUCT PLACEMENT – FLAUNT YOUR BRAND

Have you noticed in big-budget Hollywood films that you will see billboards of products and famous brand products will appear in them? I'm sure you've seen a movie or music video recently where a scene includes Beats By Dre speakers, or a bottle of well-known vodka prominently placed for the camera to pick up. This is called product placement and is an excellent way for companies and brands to expose a large audience to their products and services.

Look at the famous fragrance advertisements and clothing lines that pay celebrities and high-profile models to display their products. People love these celebrities and are eager to buy whatever they are wearing. It is basic human psychology that we want to imitate people we perceive to be more successful than us. That imitation often comes in the form of copying their clothing.

However, it's not easy to manage to persuade a celebrity to wear your t-shirts. The best you can do is contact celebrity stylists, talent agents, or the celebrities themselves via their social media accounts, on the off chance that they will show interest in your product. It may be better to wait until your brand has grown in status and achieved enough social awareness that, instead of you chasing down celebrities to wear your tees, you find them chasing you!

EXPANDING INTO RETAIL

CHAPTER 13

Your brand will grow seriously if you are able to get your collection onto the shelves of major retail outlets. This is not hard to achieve if the right tactics are used; many aspiring clothing designers see it as their ticket to super-stardom!

NOT THE SAME AS SELLING ONLINE

Many business owners these days prefer running an online-business, because they don't have to deal with customers face-to-face. It's a lot easier to handle rejection and deal with complaints via email than it is to talk them out face-to-face with a customer. However, if you plan to pursue the retail outlet path, these rejections will no longer be coming from customers but from the big bosses of retail outlets! Retail sales is online selling on steroids. You will quickly realize you are not just working to convince a customer to buy two shirts – in the retail outlet environment you will be trying to sell a business owner 100 tees or more!

It's not that difficult, really, if you approach business owners with the right attitude and some key knowledge. Equipped with these tools, the whole process can be a lot easier than expected.

It is, however, probably a good idea to wait until your brand has built up an image strong enough to grab a retail store's attention. Take a look at the following tips if or when you decide to pursue the retail path.

PIN-POINT WHAT YOU WANT

The first thing to consider is where you would like to see your brand sold, or more specifically, what outlets best fit with your brand. It is important that you are proud to see your brand sold in certain retail stores; you want into locations where your target demographic usually shops. It also helps if the style of your brand matches other similar brands sold in that specific store.

To start with, write up a list of at least twelve retail stores you can see your brand selling in, and then do some research on those stores. I'm not talking about big box stores like **Pacsun** and **Zumiez**. Start out researching smaller privately owned stores where you can meet and talk to the owner. Sometimes these stores are called boutiques. These owners are a lot easier to talk to than the big boys. They'll usually prove quite willing to work with a start-up company if you have a good quality product. If you get the owner or store buyer's email, you can always introduce yourself by sending them a brief message with your catalog or line sheet. I suggest something like:

Hi (buyer/owner's first name),

*This is (**your name**), creator of (**your brand**). We've been selling affordable shirts with great success and I think they'd be a perfect fit for (**store name**).*
- *Affordable price point for customers*
- *Awesome margins for you*
- *Guaranteed to never fade*
- *Barely take up any space*
- *No minimums and free shipping*

Can I get you started with a test order?

If you don't hear back from them, then follow up and try to connect with them preferably in person but at least on social media to show them some samples.

YOU MUST HAVE A CATALOG OR LINE SHEET

A line sheet is a sheet of paper that shows your line of t-shirts and information for making a wholesale purchase. This can also consist of a multi-page catalog. Most clothing brands will release a new catalog/line sheet every couple of months to show off their latest releases. The following will show you what you should include in your catalog/line sheet.

- **PRODUCT IMAGES** – You should use mock-ups here instead of actual photographs of the products, as they will show your design much clearer, and allow you to display close-ups of the design details without the potential problems associated with photographic close-ups.

- **PRODUCT NUMBERS** – These are important as they provide a simplified way of referring to a product instead of a lengthy and detailed verbal description. Instead of words, a series of numbers will represent specific designs. These numbers are called style numbers. For example if one of your items is a Short Sleeve (SS) shirt, then your style number will be SS01, and design 2 would be SS02 and so on.

- **LIST BOTH PRICES** – You should include both the wholesale price and the recommended retail price for your tees. Make this information easy to read and prominently located, both for yourself and your potential suppliers.

- **SHOW ALL FABRIC TYPES AND AVAILABLE COLORS**

- **MINIMUM ORDER INFORMATION** – I suggest you require a minimum order of 12 tees, and/or a minimum of 6 tees in each design type.

- **DELIVERY DATES AND CUT-OFF DATES** – It is important that the supplier knows the delivery dates and order deadlines. This gives them an idea of not only how soon they can expect to receive their orders following their purchase, but also the last day that an order may be placed.

- **YOUR CONTACT DETAILS** – Your form should include your business name, your name, as well as an email or contact number.

YOU MUST HAVE A CATALOG OR LINE SHEET (Continued)

- **ORDER FORM** – How else can the retailer make an order? You may also consider taking orders over the phone, or through a specific retailer-only section of your website. One of the biggest and most used sites for wholesale ordering is **BrandBoom.com***. You can sign up for a free account to get started. They will even call you and give you a live demo of how to use their platform to build linesheets and order forms you can send out to wholesalers. This platform is only for managing wholesale/retailer accounts, not for selling to the general public.

GIVE OUT SAMPLES

Even if your line sheet or catalog is designed with the highest quality, this still may not be enough to convince a retailer to make a purchase. There is a huge difference between holding a picture of a product, and actually getting their hands on an item. Please consider providing the retailer with a few samples of your designs so they can see the quality of your products for themselves. This is another reason why it is important to produce nothing but the highest quality of product. At this stage you will also need to convince major businesses that your product is worthy of being displayed in their stores.

If you can afford it, consider putting together a sample pack containing your line sheet/catalog, a few sample tees, and a business card for the retailers you would like to target. Try to deliver this sample pack yourself, directly into the hands of the manager or the person responsible for purchasing. You might get nine rejections, and only one successful response, but remember – you only need one major retail store to stock your product in order to become highly successful.

TERMS OF PAYMENT AND ORDERING

When a customer makes a purchase via your website, they normally pay the full amount with their credit card right away. However, when dealing with retailers and wholesale accounts, this isn't always the case. The most common payment method in this environment is called Net 30. Basically the retail/wholesale business will place an order with your company, then you have to supply the product before you get paid. This is something a lot of newbies don't understand when they want to get into retail selling. Net 30 means you have to pay out of pocket to produce the order and then require full payment within thirty days of the retailer receiving the goods. You either need to have the inventory on hand when you start selling to retail outlets, or you should have enough money in the bank to pay for the production of the goods they want to order.

Some retail outlets prefer to put you on consignment, which means they will stock your tees, but you only get paid if those tees sell. This is a method to avoid, since there is no guarantee you will get paid. Instead, push for payment before you ship the goods. That's one way to ensure that your tees have already been paid for. At the very least, request COD (Cash on Delivery), where the retailer will have to pay for the tees the moment they are received, before they are allowed to sign for receiving them.

STAYING IN CHARGE OF YOUR BRAND

CHAPTER 14

Managing a business is similar to running a car. Regular adjustments and tune-ups are required to keep the car on the road and running smoothly. Successful businesses are managed by people who are able to effectively manage their responsibilities and know when things need to be adjusted in order to keep the operation running as smoothly as possible.

SHARING RESPONSIBILITY

It is always important that you go into business with the right kind of people – people who are responsible, who share your goals and visions for the future. The best partners are people who have – or are willing to learn – skills that you may not have. They should be initiative-takers who are motivated to succeed. If you are in business with people who do not exhibit these traits, then it might be time to change up your team. You don't necessarily need to employ a large workforce of professionals; a high-quality team can consist of just two people!

It would help immensely if you are able to secure financial investments at the start of your business venture, provided by a family member or friend who was willing to become a part of your managerial team. If that didn't happen, you can still amass a dream team of your own. Make a list of family members and friends who have skills in the areas of your business that you lack or would like to grow. Another option is to look for a mentor who is willing to share with you his business savvy and experience. Skills such as graphic design, social media, accounting, or sales can help your business immensely. If you have the funds to employ individuals on a full-time basis, great. If you don't, you can always ask if she would be willing to assist you in return for a percentage of the brand's profits. Maybe your preferred friend/family would like to work a few hours each week in return for some brand new tees!

If you cannot find any assistance within your circle of family and friends, consider websites such as **partnerup.com*** and **youngentrepreneur.com***. Both are fantastic sites that allow you to network with like-minded people. For the best experience, select your dream team from among individuals located within a reasonable distance from you.

AN ARMY OF ONE

Perhaps, either by choice or because none of your family or friends are available, you have no choice but to go into business on your own. This is not a bad thing, as some of the most successful t-shirt brands in history have been based on the dedication of a single individual. However, once your business starts to grow, you will probably need to hire some support staff, because as you grow the workload will become far too heavy for one person to handle.

BRINGING NEW PEOPLE ON BOARD

When the time has come to expand your business and hire new staff members, your first step is to separate out and analyze each of the roles you currently manage yourself. At minimum, your list will probably look like this:

- Packaging orders
- Shipping
- Designing
- Printing preparation
- Blog writing ("blogging")
- Writing newsletters
- Managing social media accounts
- Customer service (phone calls and emails)
- Managing and organizing promotional events

As your business grows, you will add to this list; new roles and responsibilities will grow to the point that they can be more effectively be managed by others. The purpose of having this list on hand is that it allows you to look at functions and areas of your business from the viewpoint of what can be delegated to other people. For example, taking orders, shipping, and customer service are functions that can easily be delegated to other staff, giving you more time to apply your creative freedom to work on new designs and fresh ideas.

FREELANCERS

A freelancer is somebody who sells his/her skills on an independent contract basis. This gives freelancers the freedom to work for as many or as few clients as they choose. Freelancers can come in any form, including graphic designers, writers, film editors, photographers, and accountants. In fact, nearly every aspect of your business can be served by highly skilled freelancers who are willing to sell their services on an as-needed basis.

When hiring a freelancer, you should always see if you can view a portfolio of previous work to ensure that the person's skills match both the quality and type of work you are after. The most competitive rates come from freelancers living in developing nations such as India. To provide a comparison, a freelance graphic artist in New York may charge $1,200 compared to $300 from a designer in India.

FREELANCERS (Continued)

Ensure that both you and your freelancer clearly understand the requirements of the job in full detail. You want to avoid miscommunication from the beginning and ensure that you will receive work that matches what you initially requested. You may be required to pay 50% of the fee up front in order for a freelancer to start working on a design project. Most freelance websites, however, hold your money in Escrow until a job is successfully completed to the standard of the requested requirements. Some useful sites for connecting with freelancers are **Guru.com***, **Upwork.com***, **Behance.net***, **Coroflot.com***, and **Fiverr.com***.

DEALING WITH CUSTOMERS

One vital aspect of your business is dealing with customers and providing them with an unforgettable experience that will bring them back to your business time after time. We call this "customer service" and the ability to do this well is one of the most important aspects of your business. Customers want to be able to trust you and feel comfortable doing business with you. If you can provide them with good support, they will come back and buy from you time after time.

BEFORE THE CUSTOMER BUYS SOMETHING

You must be prepared to offer an amazing experience from the time a customer hits the inquiry stage. This stage begins the moment an individual comes in contact with you. This contact can be anything from a phone call asking about returns, to a customer visiting your website for the very first time. This is why it is extremely important for your website be attractive, easy to navigate, and equipped with a Frequently Asked Questions section (FAQs). I highly recommend including a delayed pop-up window inviting new customers to subscribe to your newsletter.

AFTER THE CUSTOMER BUYS SOMETHING

Once the customer has made a purchase, you must be able to handle all customer questions related to the processing and shipping of the order. This may be as simple as, "when can I expect to receive my order?". It is good customer service to notify the customer once the order has been shipped, including an estimated date of delivery. By doing this, your customer will feel some reassurance, since you have already taken their money.

Most shipping services provide tracking information on their websites. All you need to do is provide a link to their order on the shipper's site. That way, your customers can follow the status and location of their shipments as frequently as they want.

SHIPPING DELAYS

Every once in a while you will face issues that are completely out of your control. As soon as you are made aware of something that will impact delivery to your customers, it is important to notify them right away. It is considered extremely bad customer service to call the customer on the day they are expecting a package, only to inform them that it will take another three days... especially if you learned about the delay two days ago (BIG oops). People are much more willing to be patient with you if you are proactive in contacting them and if you share transparently what is happening.

REFUNDS, RETURNS, AND EXCHANGES

You will find customers who will purchase your tees, only to call you a few days later saying they want a refund. Customers return products for any reason, or no reason at all. A customer may not be happy with the quality, the size, the color, or they simply changed their mind. This is why you establish rules for returns, refunds, and exchanges in the first place, and why you communicate these terms clearly in multiple locations on your website. The standard policy for returns is 7 to 30 days after receiving the product for returns, provided that all tags are still in place and that the tee has not been worn.

Check up on the standard rules and conditions that currently exist in the t-shirt industry, or choose a set of reasonable rules for yourself, in which you provide terms for refunds, returns, and exchanges.

PAY SOMEBODY ELSE TO DO THE WORK

The potential exists for you to design and print your tees, and then ship them off to a fulfillment warehouse that will package, label, and ship your tees as orders come in. Not only does this save a huge amount of your time, allowing you to focus your resources and attention on other areas of your business, it also means you will not have to directly face the costs associated with storing your tees. Your profit margin can be increased. It is not recommended to contract a fulfillment warehouse to handle your orders until you are averaging at least thirty sales per month (or at least one per day).

Different fulfillment companies operate from different structures, so do your research before choosing one to do business with. These different structures may impact the costs they charge per order, storage costs, and other fees associated with the fulfillment of an order. Generally, the pricing structure looks something like this:

- Flat fee per order
- Fee per shirt per order
- Handling/small package fees
- Hand tagging fees
- Poly-bagging fees
- Storage fees (as low as $20 per month with no minimum order requirements)

On average, it may cost you between $1 and $4 per tee that is shipped through a fulfillment warehouse. I recommend you aim for $3 maximum per order just to ensure that you are not sacrificing too much of your profit margin. Before you commit to anything, compare the costs associated between using a fulfillment service and doing it yourself after hiring staff members to serve this function. Choose the most cost-effective option.

BUILDING A WORK ENVIRONMENT LIKE GOOGLE'S

Even if you are starting your t-shirt business from a back shed, the garage, or a spare bedroom, do what you can to ensure your work environment is fun and fulfilling. After all, you are going to be spending a lot of time there.

SETTING UP YOUR WORK ENVIRONMENT

The most important factor to consider when working for yourself is that you are ultimately responsible for the completion of all work inside of your business. As such, you should create a work environment free from distraction, full of inspiration, and in a bright and clean area. If you share a house with others, let them know that between 8:00am and 5:00pm, they cannot distract you, and that they should consider you to be at work like any office job. On this note, ask them to please respect your work hours and not hold loud conversations or blast the TV all day long. Both of these can be highly distracting and frustrating, and they definitely do not contribute to a healthy and inspiring workspace.

If this is not an option however, consider spending the most important hours of your workday in a place where you are guaranteed comfort and silence, like a public library. You might also consider looking online for cheap office space you can rent. Although this may cost money you would rather use for marketing, the increase in productivity could end up paying for itself in a short amount of time.

KEEP AT IT!

CHAPTER 15

No matter what arises to stand between you and your success, do not let it affect you to the point that you want to give up on your business and do something else. Try to keep finding things that motivate and inspire you to keep working toward the success you have worked so hard to achieve.

There will probably come a time when sales in your business reaches a plateau; they are just not increasing. It may seem as if your customers have lost the excitement they first showed about your brand in the early stages of development. You may feel you've lost the creative spark you had in the first stages of the design process. At this point, don't forget why you started this business in the first place. Use your starting purpose to fire up your motivation to get you through the slow zones. Whatever you do, don't give up!

If it's any consolation, nearly every successful business will have encountered this obstacle at some point in its first few months or years of growth and development. Now look at where those brands are today. Remind yourself that you have the potential to join them in the spotlight.

IDENTIFYING THE PROBLEM

If this slump in sales lasts longer than you think is normal, without any signs of improvement, it might be time to take a look at the various aspects of your business, to try and pinpoint the problem that is keeping your customers from purchasing your tees.

Your first step is to monitor the traffic on your website; you want to figure out the conversion rate you are operating on. A conversion rate can be defined as the percentage of customers who visit your website, compared to how many of them actually buy something. For example, let's say that in one day 200 people visited your website. If only 4 of these people made a purchase, then your business is operating on a conversion rate of 2%. This means you are missing out on 98% of the potential customers who visit your site. Hopefully your traffic does not reflect a conversion rate like this. However, you just might get away with this if your profit margin is good. In this case, it is obvious that something is seriously wrong.

The second thing you should do is make sure there are no technical errors on your website. Check for problems that prevent people from making a purchase or even accessing your website. If everything appears to be fine with the site's functionality, you may need to tweak your brand profile a bit.

Consider asking your site visitors what is holding them back from buying. A strategic way to do this is to design an exit pop-up window. As customers leave your website without making a purchase, ask them to check a box as to why they have not made a purchase today. The answers could be as simple as - "too hard to navigate website", "too expensive", "outdated designs", and perhaps an "other reason" option where customers can write down their own reasons.

Next, check into "abandon cart" plugins and ads. These plugins will reach out to customers who may have placed products into a shopping cart, but never checked out. This is a gentle way to remind your visitors that they once had interest in buying; hopefully they will come back and complete their purchases.

Picreel* is also a great tool to help improve conversations. Picreel recovers abandoning visitors and turn them into customers with Picreel exit intent technology. Know everything from visits to conversions with insight analytics.

IDENTIFYING THE PROBLEM (Continued)

Obtaining feedback from your customers is probably the best method to use when working out why business has dropped off. There may be any number of reasons behind the slump in sales, but you will never know unless you ask. Until you know what's amiss, you won't be able to fix the problem.

REWARD YOURSELF FOR YOUR HARD WORK

Just as employees are rewarded for their hard work through awards, promotions and weekends away, you too should be rewarded for the hard work you are putting into your business. Set yourself realistic and achievable goals, and when those benchmarks are reached, reward yourself with something like a new watch, a fancy dinner in a 5-star restaurant, or just give yourself a pat on the back. Whatever option you choose, you must believe that you have truly earned the reward and believe that you deserve that reward.

The point is that you are training yourself to be highly disciplined, so that when you are faced with obstacles you will be able to deal with them without panicking, and making quick misguided mistakes that may result in a negative impact to your business. Remember, your ultimate goals in life are nothing more than a series of smaller steps. Each step you climb brings you closer to your goals, and this equals success!

BEYOND SUCCESS

CHAPTER 16

Now that you have reached the final chapter of this book, you should have a clear understanding of what it takes to brainstorm, design, implement, manage and grow a successful t-shirt business. But, this is only the beginning of your journey.

EXPANDING YOUR PRODUCT RANGE

You will eventually reach the pinnacle of your success selling t-shirts alone, and will find it necessary to expand your product collection and offer your customers a wider array of choices if you want to stay in the business for the long run.

The next step up from designing and selling t-shirts, is to consider including sweatshirts and hoodies. These can cost anywhere from an extra $3 to $12 or more per item, but the profit margins are much higher because these items can be sold for much higher prices. Just be careful to sell them in the appropriate season (that is, don't try to sell hoodies in the middle of the summer heat, or you will be throwing money away).

If you don't feel you have the operating budget to add the additional expenses of increasing your product range through sweatshirts and hoodies, consider selling badges or stickers. They cost next to nothing to produce (a few cents in most cases), and can be sold for $2 or $3 each. If you remember the chapter where we talked about up-selling, this is a perfect opportunity to increase your operating revenue and profit margins. These smaller items are a good financial investment, because they require a very small financial output for products that have the potential to triple or quadruple your investment, depending on your selling prices.

As your funds increase, you can consider expanding your product range further into higher value items such as jackets, button-down shirts, pants, and even hats. If you look at the success that brands such as Nike and Adidas have achieved by expanding their businesses through a wide range of product options (even including fragrances!), you can capture the inspiration that will allow you to see into the future of your brand's potential.

ALIBABA.COM

Alibaba.com* is an excellent resource you can use to find new manufacturers from all over the world. From the site's search bar, type in a few keywords that best describe your product. If you can't find a match there, then it's a good chance it can not be made.

1). Look for these notices on the companies you find:
- Are they Gold Suppliers? This means the business has been assessed and registered. Try to only work with companies that have been a Gold supplier for 3-4+ years.
- Are they a Supplier Assessed? This means that virtually all aspects of the business have been checked, from the manufacturing plant to their HR practices.
- Are they Online Now? Check this early so you don't waste time emailing when you can get quotes right away.

Be careful when dealing with international suppliers. Always request a sample from at least three potential manufacturers, and then choose the one that has the highest quality product. You don't want to put in an order for several hundred sweatshirts, only to find that the stitching or sizes are not up to the high standard you require. Product images on websites do not always reflect the actual product you receive.

2). Find out:
- What is their turnaround time? Aim for 7-15 days max.
- What is their MOQ (Minimum Order Quantity)? What is the cost? Don't worry too much about price per piece right now. Just don't order more than a few pieces.
- Do they accept PayPal payments? This is pretty much the safest way to pay anyone.

Also, make sure the sample you request is a custom order, incorporating your design. It might cost two to five times more money per item to order a sample than if you ordered 25 to 100 of them, but that is a lot better than ordering 100 products straight off the bat, spending several hundred dollars, only to find out that they are substandard in quality. Spending a little money up front on a sample is a good way to know what kind of quality you will get. In this case, the money you invest is definitely worth the risk.

BRAND PARTNERSHIPS

When the time comes that you are running a successful t-shirt business, you will eventually come across other people running a similar business. These people may actually want to collaborate on designs and ideas, resulting in limited edition designs that have the potential to be showcased to a market that double your normal size. You both will be doing some cross marketing to each other's fans and customers in your market.

If this is something you would consider aiming for, consistently produce high-quality designs that will make a name for yourself and be a brand worth collaborating with. Examine thoroughly any brands that want to develop a partnership. Make sure that their company is serious and that collaboration would be mutually beneficial. The worst you can do is link up with a smaller brand that has no following and a bad product. It just wants a free ride on your success. Don't fall for that trap.

OPENING YOUR OWN RETAIL OUTLET

Once you have built your brand to a point where it is consistently making profits and filling a constant supply of orders, you may consider opening up your very own retail outlet. This can give your business both a virtual and physical presence in the marketplace. However, this avenue is not cheap; there are many costs associated with a physical shop, such as shop fittings, furniture, clothing racks, sales staff, a lease, utilities, and other associated costs. You can expect to pay a minimum ranging from $10,000 up to $100,000 to open a retail outlet worthy of your brand's reputation, especially if your dream is to have a shop on the infamous Fairfax street in Los Angeles, where companies like Supreme and Diamond Supply reside.

The second factor to consider after cost is location. If you open up your store in the suburbs, you may be lucky to get one customer a week. Look for areas that have outlets similar to yours, or set up shop in an area heavily populated by your target market and foot traffic. Consider how you have priced your shirts; check to see if the financial demographics of your area are capable of affording the price of your shirts.

We spoke earlier about stocking select sizes of shirts in your web store rather than stocking every size within that range. It is important in a retail store to maintain sufficient stock of those select sizes. If a customer comes in and you do not currently stock the size they want, they may never return and you will have missed out on a quick sale.

You should also reflect your brand image and values in the layout and presentation of your store. We spoke earlier about the importance of pulling together your themes, designs, colors, and other items. Since your store is the place you will be selling your brand, make sure you keep it within the visual profile of your brand.

Another good way to bring new customers into your store is to host events and exclusive promotions to new and existing customers. Consider starting a loyalty program, or hold 50% off sales at the beginning of each season, to immediately put you ahead of your competition. Since we already have our online store running simultaneously, our retail store can survive slow months because we can still sell our collection online around the world.

YOU MADE IT!

CONCLUSION

Here we are at the conclusion to this book. By now you should have a hungry desire to make it big in the t-shirt industry and start your very own t-shirt business. Always stay positive and focused on your goals, remembering that they are nothing but a series of smaller steps that can be accomplished on a daily basis until you reach your big dreams.

Running a t-shirt business is not easy, but you should now have a good idea of what will be required of you; you will always have this book to use as a guide, if you ever find yourself stuck or uninspired. Learn from your mistakes and don't stop until you make it. Now go out there and be successful!

RESOURCES

Domain Name Registration

Domain.com* – Register a domain name and transfer domains. Reliable web hosting and VPS. Powerful website, blog, and e-commerce tools. 12 years, millions of customers. A lot of times you can find coupons for discounts on buying domain names and hosting when you search.

HostGator* – Is a leading provider of web hosting, VPS hosting and dedicated servers. Discover why over 9,000,000 websites trust them to meet their hosting needs.

Bluehost* – Is one of the largest and most trusted web hosting services, powering millions of websites.

Website Comprehensive Platforms

Shopify* – While many of the features involve extra fees, Shopify is one of the most flexible shopping cart programs available and is designed to grow with your business needs. It has excellent security, a good interface and strong features that, combined with educational support for your business, make Shopify an excellent choice for e-commerce software. ($19-$180 a month)

Big Cartel – Is home to nearly a million clothing designers, bands, record labels, jewelry makers, crafters, and other artists. ($10-$30 a month)

Bigcommerce* –Very similar to Shopify in terms of core features but tends to focus on more established merchants. Software is easy to use and full of features to manage your business and promote sales. In addition, Bigcommerce goes beyond the online store to provide you with additional support and information to help make your e-commerce business a success. ($29.95 a month)

Website Comprehensive Platforms (Continued)

Wordpress / Woo Commerce* – Is a free e-commerce plugin that allows you to sell anything, beautifully. Built to integrate seamlessly with WordPress, WooCommerce is the world's favorite e-commerce solution that gives both store owners and developers complete control.

Specialty Platform Recommendations

Gumroad* – Gumroad can be used to sell physical items, digital downloads – quickly and easily – direct from your website or via social media. Does not support the selling of services (consulting).

Selz* – Selz can be used to sell physical items, digital downloads, and services – quickly and easily – direct from your website or via social media.

CrateJoy* – Want to sell a subscription product? Check out CrateJoy. Their platform is built specifically for the intricacies that surround a subscription-based product.

Merchant Services

Paypal* – Is the faster, safer way to send money, make an online payments, receive money or set up a merchant account.

Amazon Payments* – Is a fast, easy and safe way to accept payments online and on mobile.

Square* – Is one service for your entire business, from secure credit card processing - including Apple Pay & EMV - to point of sale solutions.

Design Software

Adobe Photoshop – Create incredible images using the world's best photo editing software. ($9 a month)

Adobe Illustrator – Is a vector graphics editor and is the industry standard for designing. ($9 a month)

FotoFuze* – Make professional product photography out of ordinary photographs from ordinary cameras for free.

Design Software (Continued)

Pixlr* – A free online image editor. Allows you to fix, adjust, and filter images in a browser.

Pixc* – Will remove the background from your product images within 24 hours. With Pixc, you just take a photo of your products and upload it through the Pixc dashboard. Your images will come back to you within 24 hours, touched up and with a crisp white background.

Linesheets & Wholesale Ordering

BrandBoom* – Create line sheets for free and present your products to retail buyers. Collect wholesale orders online and manage them in one place.

NuOrder* – B2B/Wholesale e-commerce solutions for buyers & brands. NuORDER's 2-way ordering system takes your business digital 24/7, bringing your selling to the next level.

Finding Designers, Photographers, and Models

Dribbble* – Is a web-app based on the dribbble.com website which was created to improve and simplify your inspirations using the best designers in the world.

Behance.net* – Showcase and discover the latest work from top online portfolios by creative professionals across multiple industries.

Coroflot* – A career and community site hosting individual creative portfolios, a global design firm directory, and a database of job and project openings.

Model Mayhem* – Is the #1 portfolio website for professional models and photographers. Create a profile, upload your photos and connect with other professionals.

Custom Goods – Drop Shippers

Printful* – Prints and sends custom print designs to your customers for products such as t-shirts, posters, canvas, mugs etc.

Scalable Press* – Is an on-demand t-shirt fulfillment service that offers DTG, screen printing, and fulfillment from three state-of-the-art production facilities.

Screen Printers

Taggler – Custom apparel ordered and delivered in five easy steps. Uploading your design and posting your order takes only a few minutes. You'll then receive quotes.

Threadbird* – Custom printed t-shirt & apparel experts specializing in high-quality discharge, water based and plastisol prints for brands.

Jak Prints* – Is a premier print shop with over a decade of experience in online printing. Get custom shirts, business cards, and more.

Mammoth Printing* – Is a full-service screen printing facility with over 18 years of printing experience.

Social Media Tools

Archie* – Archie is like having a $9/month social media employee. Archie allows you to see hash tags and keywords to auto-favorite/like on both Instagram and Twitter which can help you grow your profile and brand exposure exponentially and passively.

Sniply* – The problem with sharing links on social media is that most of the time you're sending people away from your site. Sniply fixes that by adding a layer on top of every page you share with a call to action to help bring some people back to your site.

Edgar* – At $49/month, Edgar is on the pricey side. Edgar is the only app that allows you to build out a library of updates/shares/tweets. Edgar then allows you to schedule your updates but the key difference is that it will keep using the library over and over again so you don't have to keep rescheduling evergreen content.

Pagemodo – Is like Edgar but doesn't cost as much. At $33/month it helps you edit Facebook cover photos, make custom tabs, schedule and design your social media posts and create contests for Facebook. You can also link it to your twitter account and it helps supply content for you to post.

Hootsuite* – Enhance your social media management with Hootsuite, the leading social media dashboard. Manage multiple networks and profiles and measure your engagement.

Product Sourcing

Alibaba* – Find quality manufacturers, suppliers, exporters, importers, buyers, wholesalers, products, and trade leads from Alibaba's award-winning International Trade Site.

Makers Row* – Makers Row is an amazing directory of over 7,000 American manufacturers. If you're looking to have a product manufactured in the USA, this is unequivocally your first stop.

Examine China* –The problem with Alibaba is that it is riddled with scammers. Not sending the products, lack of proper certificates, money fraud, sending sand or trash in containers, and fake accounts are just some of the frauds Examine China can protect you from. Examine China sends you a detailed report in PDF format, containing all trusted and credible data on the Chinese company.

Store Themes

Out of The Sandbox* – This is a great Shopify theme developer. They invest a lot of quality, attention to detail, and support into every single one of their handcrafted themes.

Theme Fiend* – Provides high quality Big Cartel and Shopify themes for all types of merchants. Check out our selection of online store themes.

Template Monster* – Is a website that sells mainly website templates like WordPress Themes, HTML Templates and flash templates etc.

Themeforest* – Browse top selling WordPress Themes & Templates on ThemeForest. This list updates weekly with the top selling and best themes.

Creative

AppSumo* – Sign up to the newsletter list and wait for amazing free or significantly discounted apps and tools to help you grow your business.

CreativeMarket* – Buy and sell handcrafted, mouse-made design content like vector patterns, icons, photoshop brushes, fonts and more.

Creative (Continued)

TailorBrands* –Using advanced machine learning and powerful algorithms, Tailor Brands will analyze your brand's name, values and industry and will create a series of unique logos and brand identities within minutes that you can choose from.

Store Apps & Tools

BOLD Apps* – There's lots of Shopify App in the Shopify App Store, however, they are not all built equal. BOLD Apps is one of Shopify's closest 3rd party partners, and for good reason. BOLD Apps is a Shopify exclusive agency that builds some incredible, stable, and useful apps that extend the functionality of your Shopify store. With over 20 apps (all of them have a 5 star rating!) you're sure to find one to help solve a problem you're facing.

Picreel* – Recover abandoning visitors and turn them into customers with Picreel exit intent technology. Know everything from visits to conversions with insight analytics.

Gleam* – Normally there's no reason for someone who enters your contest to share it. It actually decreases their chance of winning. Gleam changes that by increasing participants' chances of winning by sharing. This allows you to create mega-viral contests and drive massive new traffic to your store.

Email Marketing

MailChimp* – Free for your first 2,000 email subscribers. The default and easiest to use email marketing tool. MailChimp is the standard and because of that, MailChimp integrates with everything else and everything else integrates with MailChimp.

Klaviyo* – Is an email service for making more money. The best part is that Klaviyo is free for your first 250 contacts.

Constant Contact – You can create effective email marketing and other online marketing campaigns to meet your business goals.

SEO Tools

SEMrush* – Is a powerful and versatile competitive intelligence suite for online marketing, from SEO and PPC to social media and video advertising research.

SEO Review Tools* – A suite of free tools to help you with your content and SEO strategy. Check backlinks, page authority, and site authority. Just simple, effective and free SEO tools that work.
Packaging

Packaging & Stickers

Sticker Giant* – Get quality custom stickers and labels printed fast and shipped free, made right here in America.

Pakible* – Lets you create your own custom packaging the easy way. Design online, in quantities as low as 10, right to your door.

Uline – Probably one of the biggest packaging suppliers on the planet. A thousand choices for boxes and other packaging material at fair prices. The best starting point for all of your packaging needs.

Shipping & Fulfillment | Shipping & Label Printing Apps

Shippo* (Beginner) – The simplest and easiest shipping label app. When you connect it to your store, orders are automatically imported. Just enter the package size and weight and print off your shipping label from one of their shipping partners (USPS, Canada Post, FedEx, UPS). No monthly fees. Each label costs the price of postage plus 5 cents.

ShippingEasy* (Beginner) – Free if you're shipping less than 50 orders per month. ShippingEasy allows you to print shipping labels and gets you exclusive access to carrier rates normally reserved for companies shipping 50,000+ packages per month.

ShipStation* (Intermediate) – Shipping higher volume? ShipStation is likely your answer. With integrations with over 60 platforms and marketplaces and over 300 reviews (mostly all 5 stars), ShipStation is a favorite merchant shipping platform. ShipStation starts at $25/month for up to 500 orders/month.

Recommended Fulfillment Warehouses

Shipwire* (Worldwide Warehouses) – They have no minimums and provide direct integration with Shopify, so getting started is pretty easy. Shipwire has a pricing calculator on its site which is nice for getting an idea of costs. Shipwire doesn't own any of its warehouses. It is more of a software solution that rents space from other warehouses. This can cause issues if you have custom requests or specialty needs.

ThinkLogistics* (Canada Based) – Based in Canada and looking for a top of the line fulfillment warehouse? ThinkLogistics is one of the few fulfillment warehouses in North America that uses KIVA robots to assist in the order fulfillment process. The team here is great and you'll have an account manager that can help you with any special requests, or custom packaging. An app for Shopify makes this a great option for Canadian e-commerce entrepreneurs.

Fulfillrite* (USA East Coast Based) – Fulfillrite is a New Jersey-based, family owned fulfillment warehouse. Fulfillrite is a great choice for any small to medium sized retailer. Fulfillrite integrates with all major and modern e-commerce services (Shopify, Bigcommerce, Amazon, Squarespace, Etsy, and dozens more).

Recommended Customs Broker

Pacific Customs Broker* – If you plan on importing products from another country (like China), you'll need a reliable customs broker. A customs broker acts on your behalf to help you bring your goods into the country (USA, Canada). They will complete the necessary paperwork and obtain all the licenses for you.

Tradeshows

Agenda* – Is a forum for the most inspired in the streetwear and action sports industries to unite. Three shows a year in Long Beach, New York, and Las Vegas.

The Bank Sale* – Street & Contemporary Fashion Expo in Los Angeles.

ISS* (Imprinted Sportswear Show) – Is the largest trade show dedicated to the decorated apparel industry. Located nationwide, attendees will find the best apparel printing vendors. Five shows a year.

Tradeshows (Continued)

Magic* – Retail buyers from around the world have descended on Las Vegas for the twice- yearly Magic Market Week, the fashion industry's largest trade show.

Venue* – The largest event of the annual L.A. Fashion Week brings Nationwide/ International buyers, press, and fashion industry insiders to the West Coast.

Legal Resources

Legal Zoom – Is the nation's leading provider of personalized, online legal solutions and legal documents for small business owners and families.

Accounting

Starter:

Shoeboxed* –Keep track of revenues (easy) and keep track of expenses (hard). Shoeboxed makes keeping track of your expenses super easy. Every time you buy something snap a photo and upload it to Shoeboxed. It will automatically log and tag it, making it super easy for you to do your taxes at the end of the year. Shoeboxed receipt scans are both IRA (U.S.A.) and CRA (Canada) approved.

Quickbooks Online –Has a lot of features and integrations that pull in data from bank & credit card accounts and will collaborate with your accountant-for an affordable monthly fee.

Xero – Is online accounting software for small businesses. Use Xero to manage invoicing, bank reconciliation, bookkeeping and more.

Intermediate/Advanced:

Bench Accounting* (U.S. Based Merchants Only) – Their plans start at $125/ month, but Bench gives you really great apps to upload all your financials and then pairs you with a real bookkeeper who provides you tax-ready financial statements. They take (almost) all the pain out of accounting.

Continued Learning Information & Advice

Skillshare* –Is a platform for learning new skills. Whether it's branding, product photography, Adobe Photoshop, or accounting, Skillshare offers great, hands-on classes taught by industry leading experts.

CreativeLive* – CreativeLive is very different from Skillshare. CreativeLive brings in the world's leading experts on topics like photography or Adobe Photoshop (or dozens of other topics) to teach live classes. The classes are free to watch live, you only pay if you want to actually buy the video recordings after you've viewed them.

Udemy – Is an online education marketplace with limitless variety: over seven million students are enrolled in more than 30,000 courses,taught by 19,000 instructors.

T-Shirt Forums* – The official friendly t-shirt forum and community to discuss custom t-shirts, starting a business, screen printing, embroidery, DTG, heat transfers, relabeling, and more.

Mintees* – Is an online t-shirt and apparel design community. It serves tee designers, clothing brands and tee enthusiasts.

Productivity

Dropbox* – Is a service that keeps your files safe, synced, and easy to share. Bring your photos, docs, and videos anywhere and never lose a file again.

Google Docs* – Brings your documents to life with smart editing and styling tools to help you easily format text and paragraphs.

Basecamp* – Is the leading web-based project management and collaboration tool. It includes to-dos, files, messages, schedules, and milestones.

Trello* – Keeps track of everything, from the big picture to the minute details.

Productivity (Continued)

Evernote* – Is an app that allows you to collect inspirational ideas, write meaningful words, and move your important tasks onto a to-do list.

Physical Products

Notebook or Sketch Book – Use this to record your ideas and to plan. It's good to have everything in one place so you can always look back.

DYMO LabelWriter 4XL Thermal Label Printer – If you're not drop shipping or at the stage of using a fulfillment warehouse, then you need to find a way to ship your orders efficiently. This is the most popular label printer and works with all postage/label printing apps so you can pack, print, and ship your orders fast.

Ozeri Touch Professional Digital Scale – In order to print your own labels you'll need to weigh your orders. With nearly 1,500 reviews and an average 4 1/2 stars, this inexpensive but effective scale should be all you need.

Square Perfect 30-Inch Light Tent for Product Photography – If you're doing your own product photography, you'll need a good backdrop to take ultra clean photos. This is my recommended light tent for taking the best product photos. It folds up nicely as well for easy storage.

Digital SLR Camera – There are lots of choices for cameras these days. Ultimately, you can use a newer smart phone, but the best photos will come from a DSLR camera.

Printed in Great Britain
by Amazon